Mary Hunt's

DEBT PROOF

YOUR

Holidays

Mary Hunt's

DEBT PROOF

YOUR Holidays

MARY HUNT

Founder and Publisher of *Cheapskate Monthly*™

BROADMAN
&HOLMAN
PUBLISHERS

Nashville, Tennessee

0-8054-1678-1

This edition published in 1998 by

Broadman & Holman Publishers, Nashville, Tennessee

Editorial team: Vicki Crumpton, Janis Whipple, Kim Overcash

Page design: Anderson Thomas Design

Typesetting: PerfecType

First edition published in 1997 by

St. Martin's Press, 175 Fifth Avenue, New York, NY 10010

Dewey Decimal Classification: 332.024

Subject Heading: FINANCE, PERSONAL/HOLIDAYS/

CHRISTMAS/CONSUMER CREDIT—UNITED STATES

Library of Congress Card Catalog Number: 98-24555

Library of Congress Cataloging-in-Publication Data

Hunt, Mary, 1948–

Mary Hunt's debt-proof your holidays / Mary Hunt.

p. cm.

ISBN 0-8054-1678-1 (pbk.)

1. Finance, Personal—United States.

2. Consumer credit—United States. 3. Christmas. 4. Holidays

I. Hunt, Mary, 1948– Cheapskate monthly debt-proof your holidays.

II. Title

HG179.H8546   1998

332.024—dc21

98-24555

CIP

1 2 3 4 5   02 01 00 99 98

Dedication

For
my friend
Kathleen Chapman,
a woman of many talents
not the least of which is the ability
to take a pile of
empty Jell-O boxes, scraps of paper,
curling ribbon, and a few twinkle lights and produce a
Christmas tree
so elegant
it defies
description.

A Note from the Author

This is a book about special holidays—not necessarily Christmas—and debt. The author celebrates Christmas, and so you will read that word often. But if you celebrate Hanukkah, Kwanzaa, or some other special holiday, these same principles, ideas, and suggestions can apply. Just make your holiday substitution each time you come to the word *Christmas*.

All references to debt in this book are to unsecured debt such as revolving credit card balances, installment loans, and personal loans. *Debt,* as it is used in this book, does not refer to secured debt such as a mortgage or auto loans.

Table of Contents

Introduction   1

PART I

Less Happy than Hassled, More Dazed than Dazzled   5

1. You Call *This* Peace on Earth?   7
2. Learn from the Past   12
3. Debt Is Not the Answer   20

PART II

Christmas by Choice, Not by Chance   **33**

4. It's a Matter of Values   35
5. Shape Your Attitudes   42
6. Commit to Cash   53
7. Develop a Plan   61
8. It's Never Too Early   68

PART III

Anti-Debt Holiday Solutions   **75**

9. Gift Ideas   77
10. Cards and Gift Wrapping   102
11. Decorating Your Home   112
12. Holiday Entertaining   127
13. Family Fun   133

PART IV

One Step Further   **147**

14. A Plan to Wipe Out Debt Forever   149

Afterword   162
Endnotes   163
A Special Offer from *Cheapskate Monthly*   164

Introduction

I love Christmas. I mean I really *love* Christmas—everything about Christmas. But it hasn't always been that way for me. There were years when anticipation far exceeded the actual event because I approached the season without limitation. Whatever felt good at the moment, whatever the kids wanted, and whatever was expected—that's what I did. And each year when it was finally over, it wasn't really over. Like that miserable bloated feeling after eating way too much, I belched my way into each new year, suffering from a horrible aftertaste as month after month the bills arrived to remind me how much I'd spent on what and how little I remembered.

Years ago there was a huge scare about the highly flammable nature of certain types of flannel fabrics. At the time I had two little babies, and I recall the chills that ran up my spine at the mere thought of them being enveloped in flames as they lay snuggled up in their flannel jammies.

I'm certain I overreacted—as I am wont to do—but my little boys didn't wear flannel after that. Even though new regulations required fabrics of this sort to be treated and labeled as

1

fire-retardant, that wasn't good enough for me. If there was even the slightest chance of a problem, I wanted a *fire-proof* label.

I wish that I would have overreacted to the dangers of the credit cards I collected in the same way I responded to the fabric. If I had, perhaps I would have avoided years of pain having to pay back horrendous amounts of money to reverse holiday damage.

Some kind of debt-retardant treatment would have been nice. Better yet, I wish I would have been debt-proofed with some kind of Teflon-type material so the temptation to accept easy credit would not have stuck. But I wasn't and it did and as a result I've learned an awful lot over the past years.

I have yet to find a way to dip us into some magical substance so that we won't be tempted by consumer credit. But I have come up with a plan that when followed will have the effect of *debt-proofing* the one single event during the year that has the greatest possibility of throwing us into a financial tailspin.

What I have for you is a debt-proof plan and hundreds of fantastic ideas and suggestions for everything from entertaining to decorating to gift-giving that will help you discover and develop your own solutions.

My debt-proof plan for your Christmas holidays is not at all complicated. On the contrary, it is logical and easy to follow. It is not a one-size-fits-all solution because our individual lives are as different as our individual desires, abilities,

Introduction

and means. This plan will help simplify the season so that you will have more time to reflect and celebrate the reason—the birth of our Savior, Jesus Christ.

So here's the deal: I'll provide the information, and you provide the commitment. We're going to make a great team; so, let's get going. Prepare yourself for the most meaningful Christmas you and your family have ever experienced—a very merry, debt-free Christmas!

Think of this book as a solution if

🎁 Christmas is for you the happiest and the most stressful time of the year.

🎁 your Christmas bills always last longer than the season.

🎁 you can't imagine Christmas shopping without your credit cards.

🎁 your kids have developed high expectations and you feel there's no way you could ever disappoint them at Christmas.

🎁 you never intend to go nuts with the credit cards but Christmas can be so overwhelming.

🎁 there's never enough money to do things the way you'd like.

🎁 you feel pressured to transform your home into a Christmas wonderland that will dazzle friends and family with your creativity, elegance, and grace.

DEBT-PROOF YOUR HOLIDAYS

🎁 every December 26 you make the same promise: Next year I'll start earlier, do less, enjoy more, and not use the credit cards.

🎁 you seem to have a short memory because the pattern of overdoing, overspending, and overdebting seems to repeat itself every year.

Part I

LESS HAPPY THAN HASSLED, MORE DAZED THAN DAZZLED

Chapter 1

You Call *This* Peace on Earth?

The trouble with Christmas is not that it has become overcommercialized—tell me what part of our lives hasn't? The trouble with Christmas is we allow it to get the better of us. We treat it as a contest or final examination rather than a time of rest, reflection, and joy.

In our *fantasies,* Christmas comes into our lives like a horse-drawn sleigh, decorated with pine boughs and bells. As it glides to our doorstep, we're invited to climb aboard as we are handed the reins to the mighty team of Clydesdales. As we direct this thing of beauty through the crisp, sparkling holidays, the only sounds we hear are the clippety-clop of horses' hooves and the jingling of sleigh bells. The sights and sounds are breathtaking. We visit friends and loved ones, exchange perfect gifts, indulge in warm and meaningful con-versations. Our grateful children frolic in the snow, amazed by the generosity of the season.

DEBT-PROOF YOUR HOLIDAYS

We sing familiar carols, reflect on childhood memories, and rest more than we work. Every night we sit around the fireplace sipping hot cider. Our bodies and souls are refreshed as we arrive at Christmas Day with grateful hearts.

The day is spent enjoying sumptuous food and basking in the joy of being together with friends and relatives. We participate in family traditions that bring us more joy and satisfaction than we ever thought possible.

In *reality,* Christmas comes roaring into our lives like an eighteen-wheeled, supercharged, nitrous-burning, straight-six, diesel-powered, self-propelled juggernaut of a Big Rig. It pulls up, yells for us to get on board, and instructs us to find a seat in the rear. We hang on for dear life, knowing we'll have no say on how this thing will get us to where we have to be in less than a month as the number of shopping days left till Christmas blinks in headache-inducing neon lights. It doesn't take long to realize this is going to be a wild ride.

The thirty days between Thanksgiving and Christmas become a blur as we tear through town, feeling obligated to stop at every turn to decorate, shop, clean, cook, bake, wrap, send, and referee. The rig is programmed to go faster and faster because there is so little time and so many miles to cover before the journey's end.

As hard as we try to ignore it, this machine needs fuel and lots of it—and credit cards have become the combustible of choice. We are terrified at how often we need to refuel.

You Call *This* Peace on Earth?

With so many mandatory parties, pageants, and projects, we find little time to sleep. We feel ourselves being consumed by guilt and obligation, so we try to counteract those feelings by charging (we hope it's deferred billing) bigger and better gifts and buying the approval and adoration of parents and children by taking on the role of Christmas magician.

As we enter the final laps, we give up trying to conserve on the fuel because the only thing that matters is getting there before midnight on Christmas Eve. At the eleventh hour, we screech across the finish line. Our bodies exhausted and our spirits spent, we are thrown out into the snow as Big Rig screams out of our lives. And none too soon.

But instead of hearing the lovely strains of "May Your Days Be Merry and Bright" as the Big Rig disappears into the distance, we hear only threats of "I'll Be Back!"

No doubt about it, celebrating Christmas in the 1990s is a far cry from what it was even thirty years ago, thanks to the evolution of consumer credit. No longer must we concern ourselves with whether there's enough money to buy and do all that our hearts desire. Credit card companies have made it quite socially acceptable to have it all whether we can afford it or not. Little by little, we've allowed ourselves to have what we want now and worry about paying for it later.

The more we have, the more we want; the more we get, the more we need to feel satisfied. It seems that no matter how fantastic Christmas was last year, we are compelled to make it even bigger and better this year.

Fuel! Holiday extravagance comes down to a matter of fuel, and plastic has become the fuel of choice when it comes to Christmas in America. The cost is staggering.

How staggering? Check this out: In the 26 days between Thanksgiving and Christmas 1996, American consumers charged a whopping 131.4 billion dollars on their credit cards—an all-time high, up 13 percent from the previous year.[1] While some of these charges were repaid within the grace periods, more than 70 billion dollars went on to become revolving debt—plunging those credit card holders who can least afford it into even deeper financial bondage.

When it's all said and done, it seems the entire gift-giving process—which is what really started all of this in the first place—has become all but divorced from the actual impulse, from the love or the kindness. It's just shopping; it's just money; it's just crossing names off lists and moving on.

As a child I recall my dad comparing his childhood Christmases to ours. His "I was lucky to get an orange and a few nuts for Christmas" speech was a tradition around our house. And his point? To contrast how overindulged we were with how deprived he had been. I rolled my eyes then, but every now and again the simplicity of such a time does hold a certain charm.

You Call *This* Peace on Earth?

Look, I'm not suggesting that we return to the piece-of-citrus-and-a-couple-of-pecans standard. Nor am I suggesting that we can transform our Big-Rig-holidays into charming carefree sleigh rides. What I am suggesting is that it's possible to stand back, evaluate, and then come up with a plan by which our expectations are realistic, our efforts provide satisfaction, and everything is paid in full.

Chapter 2

Learn from the Past

If past Christmases have left you in debt and less than satisfied, now's the time to evaluate what went wrong and make changes to prevent repeat performances. If you don't learn from the mistakes you've made in past years, it's likely you'll keep doing the same things year after year—and keep paying for them month after month for many years to come.

I'll never forget the year I had a very ambitious idea to host a Christmas boutique in our home. Our boys were toddlers, so it must have been nearly twenty years ago—long before this kind of boutique-in-the-living-room thing was as popular as it is nowadays.

I've always enjoyed crafts, and the thought of turning our house into a little country store for one weekend in early December sounded like a lot of fun. With any luck I'd end up with enough cash to pay for Christmas.

12

Learn from the Past

I invited a few crafty-types to participate, and the word traveled quickly. Before I knew it I'd agreed to accept more than fifteen different individuals and businesses to participate.

From the moment I decided to go through with this quasi-commercial venture, I became obsessed with the details. Because of the sheer volume of merchandise involved, I decided to relocate our furniture to the garage and basically move out of the greater portion of our house.

I knew this sale would be a huge money-maker if it was properly advertised and the products were elegantly and uniquely displayed. For this I would need lots of supplies. I felt quite justified in putting these expenses on credit. "It takes money to make money" was my motto. I'd march right down to the credit card company and pay it all off the moment the boutique closed. Right.

I'm told the event was quite a hit. People were lined up around the block long before opening time on the first morning. During the four-day event, many hundreds of people patronized my boutique, the first of its kind in our community.

While the entire event remains mostly a blur, I do know that I overplanned, overprepared, overworked, overspent, and overexpected. Basically I made a fool of myself.

My best memory of the event is that it ruined my life. I went way overboard and devoted every bit of energy I had to preparation and recovery. I still feel the pangs of burnout as I reflect on it.

DEBT-PROOF YOUR HOLIDAYS

Never once did I consider repeating the idea, which is a shame because it was quite successful. Had I taken the time to analyze systematically what I did wrong, what I did right, what I could do to fix the wrongs and repeat the rights, there is an excellent possibility I could have salvaged the idea and turned it into a seasonal cottage industry.

The only time I ever think about my short-lived holiday boutique now is when I find myself browsing through someone else's unique store. I experience a small twinge of regret when I think that this might have been mine.

Most of us don't have the option of banishing Christmas from our lives, as I did with my boutique, simply because it's been disastrous in the past. That's why the step of *evaluation* is of the utmost importance in taking back control.

To begin the process of evaluation answer the following questions thoughtfully and honestly as they relate to Christmases past. It would be good to get a notebook and write down your answers because you will want to refer to your responses later on in chapter 7. As you consider these questions, don't let guilt and fear enter the picture. You are only evaluating at this point, so step back and assess the situation with your head, not your heart. Think of yourself as a paid consultant who has been brought into a corporation to look at ways to make the company more efficient and more profitable.

What holiday factors caused you to overspend? The possibilities are numerous: gift-giving, entertaining, decorating, guilt, peer pressure, family pressure, influence of magazine photo spreads and articles (remember that gingerbread village that looked so cute and was said to be easy-enough-to-complete-in-just-one-evening?), television ads, mail-order catalogs, desire for acceptance and approval, expectations of others, fear you might leave someone out, the family photo session, Christmas cards, gift wrapping, shipping costs, fear of appearing too cheap, fear of hurting someone's feelings, wanting to make Christmas perfect for your children, attempting to re-create your own childhood, trying to compensate for an absent parent, leaving too much to the last minute.

What were the factors that caused the most stress and pressure? School parties, community events, neighborhood activities, entertaining overnight guests, decorating your home inside and out, church activities, leaving gift-making and shopping to the last minute, being responsible for too many activities outside of the home, long Christmas lists from the children, elaborate dinner parties, meeting other's expectations, too little money, not feeling appreciated, wanting to measure up to other's expectations, the office parties and related politics, or wasting all that money on the ingredients for the gingerbread village the magazine said could be made and assembled in one evening.

As you look back on Christmas last year, what do you wish you had done more of? Spending more time with the kids, playing more games, putting together a jigsaw puzzle, relaxing more, spending more time with your spouse and close friends, doing more baking, doing more cooking, sleeping, sitting in front of the fire and reading an entire book, watching *It's a Wonderful Life* all the way through, taking an entire afternoon to look at pictures and videos from Christmases past, attending church services and singing all of the verses of your favorite Christmas carols, making a trip into the city just to soak up the sights, bringing gifts to the kids at the shelter, riding in a horse-drawn sleigh through the snow, staying home on Christmas Eve and Christmas Day to start your own family traditions.

What do you wish you had done less of? Mindless shopping, pageant producing, party planning, baking, cleaning, cooking, shopping, float building, card writing, worrying, decorating, running around, meeting other's expectations, going to too many places on Christmas Eve *and* Christmas Day just to keep everyone else happy.

What gift problems did you encounter? Spending too much, buying extra gifts just in case you forgot some-one, giving gifts of obligation, over-gifting your children, buying to relieve guilt, second-guessing first purchases, impulse and panic buying, indulging in mail-order catalogs and the Home Shopping Network, making poor choices, not returning mistakes, losing receipts, paying expensive shipping costs.

Learn from the Past

What time problems did you encounter? Too little time spent with the children, too much time devoted to outside organizations and activities, wasted trips to the mall to find a suitable gift for the boss, too little time spent planning family activities, not enough time left to do really important things.

What activities and events would you eliminate if you could do last Christmas over again? Parties, pageants, cookie exchanges, making gifts, trips to too many relatives' homes, Christmas cards, formal photo sessions, singing in the choir for all nine Christmas Day services.

In what ways are you still paying for the expensive efforts of last Christmas? Credit card bills, installment loans, soured relationships, wounded spirits, holiday burnout, acute embarrassment, gifts promised but unfinished or not yet delivered.

Of all the holiday responsibilities and tasks you were responsible for last year, which ones could have been assigned to some other person or family member? Making gifts, decorating the house, helping with school activities, making travel arrangements, sending cards and/or family newsletter, wrapping gifts, baking cookies, preparing for houseguests, getting the tree, mailing packages, assembling toys on Christmas Eve.

Of all the holiday activities and events you and your family participated in last year, which ones might have been scaled down without any negative effect? Shopping trips, office parties, neighborhood events, community and church activities, housecleaning, visiting too many places on Christmas Eve or Christmas Day, extra grocery shopping, making cards, sending cards, sewing clothes, making gifts, decorating every square inch of the property in an effort to win the neighborhood lighting contest.

In what ways did you overestimate your time and abilities? Buying the supplies and planning to make quilts for all fifty-seven people on your shopping list, offering to deliver all the gifts on Christmas Eve for the outreach project at church, agreeing to participate in fifteen cookie-exchange parties, volunteering to plan all four children's school holiday parties, hosting Christmas dinner for ninety-eight dear friends and relatives, staying up all Christmas Eve night to perform "some assembly required" tasks.

What situations or events caused you to depend on your credit cards for holiday relief? Buying ready-made gifts two days before Christmas for all fifty-seven people on the list when the quilt plans fell through, finding a $0 balance in the checkbook as you were standing in line at the grocery store the day of the party, not wanting to disappoint the kids when you finally found exactly five tickets to Holiday on Ice, feeling so sad about the family being separated that you sent cousin Butch an airline ticket at the last minute, hiring a housecleaning service to come in while you're delivering the outreach project gifts, feeling guilty at the last minute because you didn't get your spouse gifts equal in value to what you hope he or she got you.

Okay, those are all the questions I have right now. How many sheets of paper have you filled? The more the better because that means you really put some thought into it. If you simply skimmed the questions, please go back and do the work.

I hope this exercise got you thinking in ways you've never thought before and that what you've learned about yourself will stick with you for at least a couple more chapters when we'll put this information to work.

Chapter 3
Debt Is Not the Answer

I've had plenty of experience with debt—huge amounts of nonmortgage, consumer debt, the kind of debt that is unsecured and granted on one's signature alone.

My situation was so terrible that my life was nearly ruined by the fear of losing everything that was really important to me—all because of my love affair with credit cards.

Of course I didn't keep records or detailed accountings of my spending. That would have forced me to face my debting patterns, and that's about the last thing I had in mind. I do know that a big portion of the combined consumer debt that grew each year was a result of my holiday spending.

Year after year I would promise my husband, "I'm not going to charge Christmas this year!" But I always did because I didn't have a plan for doing things differently from the years before. I was stuck in a terrible rut. I'd live as though Christmas didn't exist until December rolled around, and then it would be too late to plan ahead. In fact, I barely had time to contact all our credit card companies to request that our credit limits be extended.

Every year became worse than the year before. As our family grew, so did our gift list, our standards, our desires, our reputation, our expectations, and our kids' expectations. I got caught up in the flawed theory that I had to give the best, do the best, decorate the best, bake the best, and be the best in order to meet some basic minimum standard. I couldn't do that without money, and because we had none to spare, I believed that credit cards were our only choice. And every year after we'd blown it again, we would say the same thing: This is absolutely the last time. *Forever.* Right.

My point—and yes, I do have one—is that when it comes to debt and Christmas, I've been there, done that. And I know it's not a simple matter to stop paying for the holidays with plastic. It may not be simple—but it is possible! More than that, if you stick with me to the end of this book, I daresay it's probable that you can get through your next holiday season without incurring new debts.

Let's say, for example, that in 1997 you charged $897 on the holidays (the average on gifts in 1996, excluding holiday entertaining, decorations, and travel, according to the American Express Retail Index[2]). Sounds like a lot, perhaps, but believe me, if you knew exactly what you spent on *everything*—gifts, food, postage, shipping, entertainment, office parties, etc.—that amount may be much less than you actually shelled out.

Think back. Did you consider the long-term effect of that $897 debt, or did you simply kick yourself around the block on January 1 because, once again, you went way overboard? Likely you tried not to think about the larger payments you'd face all year long and just placed the matter in the back of your mind.

What if you continue putting your holiday expenses on credit cards? In 1998 you'll be paying for 1997. In 1999 you'll be paying for 1997 and 1998. In 2000 you'll be paying for 1997, 1998, and 1999. And you'll be committed for many, many years hence.

There's got to be a better way! There is, and I'm going to show it to you.

Debt Is Horrible

Unless you are convinced that credit card debt is horribly unthinkable and destructive to your joy, happiness, and peace of mind, you may be sitting on the fence on this whole matter of how bad revolving credit can be. So let me demonstrate just how horrible it is.

Suppose you had no unsecured debt (credit card balances, installment loans, or personal loans) on December 1, 1997. You picked up several credit cards during the year and decided to do the holidays up right for your friends, family, and yourself. You charged that infamous amount of $897 at 19.8

percent interest, minimum monthly payments of $15 or 3 percent of the outstanding balance, whichever is greater. Here's the result in black-and-white—something the credit card company will never reveal:

Loan Amount: $897
Interest Rate: 19.8 percent
Term to Payoff: 92 months
Minimum Monthly Payment: $15
Total Interest: $717.14
Total Principal: $897
Total Cash Outlay: $1,614.14

It looks like a bunch of numbers, so you just skipped down to this paragraph, right? Allow me to go back and interpret this information for you:

If you charged $897 on your credit cards at the terms outlined above, you will pay on those by-now-meaningless purchases for the next 7 years, 8 months, and you will pay the company $717.14 for the privilege! In our example, you started this buying-on-credit act on December 1, 1997, so it will be about July 1, 2005 that you'll finish paying for Christmas 1997. Is that sick?

Let me make it even worse: In 1998 you repeat the $897-on-the-credit-cards because you have so little available cash due to that huge credit card bill from the previous year. Fortunately for you (that's what the credit card companies want you to believe—that you are fortunate to have a card from them), the terms have remained the same, so you get to pay for 1998's holiday splendor for the next 7.5 years, which will put your payoff date sometime mid-2006.

Next year the same thing happens. Somehow you manage to keep your holiday spending to a "mere" $897, which you place on credit limits that have been generously extended by the credit card companies, thereby assuring the company you will remain a golden-egg-laying goose for them through 2007 and likely many years beyond. They've hooked you! You're theirs forever, so to speak, and they couldn't be more delighted.

Congratulations, you've successfully entered the world of *perma-debt,* that state where your lack of discipline and understanding has said it's OK to have today what you will somehow pay for in the future.

Debt is worse than horrible. It puts the borrower in a position of servitude to the lender. The credit card companies don't care if you are able to afford those high payments and all that interest; they won't care either if you lose your job or your spouse before the end of all those 7.5 year periods.

Your home could be destroyed in a flood along with everything you own, and do you think they will, in an act of compassion, cancel the balance of all your holiday shopping sprees? Don't count on it! You are, in a manner of speaking, their prisoner, and you will work out your sentence to the bitter end. And believe me, it will be bitter. And more than likely it will never end.

Sneaky Tactics and Devious Tricks

Retailers know a lot about their customers. The industry as a whole spends millions, possibly billions, of dollars to study the buying habits, psyche, and propensities of you and me, the buying public. They also know that the business they do during the month of December will represent about half of the year's total revenues. They're under a lot of pressure, and they bring out all of the big guns to make sure the buying public boosts their profits to levels of expectation.

The real bottom line is that they're out to separate us from our money. And they'll stop at very little in order to accomplish that.

Retailers know that if we can be convinced to buy on credit, we'll be less careful about finding the best deal, and that we will spend at least 30 percent more than if we were paying with cash. I believe most of us will spend far more than that if, in some way, we can convince ourselves we're getting away with something, that we are beating the system and getting something for free. (At least, that's the way it feels to me when I go into a store with five dollars in my pocket, buy two hundred dollars worth of stuff charged on a piece of plastic, and have the same five dollars in my pocket when I leave.)

The retail industry has come up with all kinds of gimmicks to help us past those moments of indecision. Should I charge this or pay cash? Should I get it now or wait until I can save up the money? Here are some of their sneaky tactics:

Deferred Billing

What they say: Charge it now, and we won't bill your account until . . . (typically it's six to twelve months down the road). It sounds really good because if they don't charge your account they can't charge you interest. In your mind you're assured of no interest until some time in the by-and-by when, of course, you'll have so much money you'll just pay the balance in full. You'll use their money for that time period instead of using your own (the implication being that your money is sitting in some huge, interest-bearing investment account and you're taking full advantage of the poor sucker company just like millionaires who make their millions using other people's money). And if you believe that, you've played right into their hands.

What they know: You will be tempted to place on credit something you couldn't possibly afford to pay for with cash. What's more, you'll purchase the larger model or the more expensive alternative because six or twelve months sounds so long and so far away. And you will be aided in your decision by this little voice telling you this is a wise financial move because you are beating this company at their own game. Ha-ha!

What will happen: These companies aren't stupid. They've thought this through, tested, tested, and retested. They're out to make money, folks—not sacrifice their bottom line in order for you and your family to have a wonderful holiday. They know, without a doubt, that you will buy more and go further overboard if they can make you think you're getting away with something. After all, deferred billing won't show up on the statement until July or next November, so your spouse will never find out what you charged, and, by then, you can easily slip into denial. It will be so neat, so slick, you won't have to worry your pretty little head about it until some other day, some other time . . . hopefully in some other galaxy far, far, away.

This is a really slick scheme, and you'll be ashamed of yourself if you fall for a deferred billing scam.

Zero Interest, Zero Down Payment, Zero Payments

I must admit I had a hard time figuring this one out. It just doesn't make sense that any company would allow us to fill our homes with furniture, appliances, stereos, televisions, mattresses, and who-knows-what-else with nothing down, zero percent interest, and no payments for months—sometimes years. What gives?

I decided to go straight to the source and find out, and here's the scoop: First a customer must have excellent credit to qualify (*pristine* is what one credit executive told me). Right there the company is reducing its exposure to risk significantly because most people with pristine credit would never think of buying on credit in the first place. Next, the customer must sign a contract that offers very unfavorable terms: a very high interest rate of up to 25 percent in some states with a provision that *if* the customer abides by all of the rules, that amount of interest will be forgiven for the initial term. However, if the customer fails to pay the balance in full at the end of the deferred period of time (six months is typical), even five minutes over, then that huge interest rate kicks in and is effective from day one. These companies know that 80 percent of the people who can be enticed to fall for this scam will not be able or willing to pay it off in the required time (things happen, you know), and so who's the winner? The company! And they've managed to land a new customer with a very good credit report (low risk, remember?) who will be paying huge interest rates for a whole lot of years.

Happy Holidays, Skip a Payment!

If you're carrying credit card balances, you've likely received notification (usually at holiday time) that because you are such a wonderful customer, the company is willing to forego a portion of their income in order that you—

their favorite client—can have an even merrier Christmas. The message: Go ahead and skip your payment this month. So, do you really believe they're doing you any favors? Not on your life; *read the fine print*. You see, the payment you don't make, including the interest you should have paid, is added onto the balance. So, next month your outstanding balance will have grown, just as if you'd made a purchase. But guess what? You didn't, and you have nothing to show for this "gift" from them except a bigger balance and a larger payment. Now tell me, what kind of a gift was *that*?

Debt Ensnares Us

Debt takes away options. If you run up debts today with the thought that you'll pay for all that stuff later, you're doing more than deferring payment. You're giving up options in the months and years to come.

I can't begin to relate to you all of the horror stories I have read in the hundreds of letters I've received over the past years. These are letters from people who are struggling with debts, and they have written to me to find help in solving these problems. The bondage that debt places on its victims is real, and it can be brutal. I've seen debt destroy marriages and blow families apart. I've received letters from prisoners, both male and female, who are serving time because their debts became so overwhelming they felt compelled to embezzle or engage in other crimes as their solution for keeping ahead of the monster.

The scenarios are always different, and they do not always involve secrecy, but the effects are similar. Our debts are so high we're always broke; we just can't seem to get ahead because there's always an emergency that makes us extend credit card balances to the limit. We'd love to get out from under these huge car payments, but we don't have any money to buy a replacement car for cash; if only we didn't have all these credit card payments every month, we could stop living on the edge; if only we weren't so far into debt, we could really start saving for the future. If only . . .

In the beginning, debt appears so innocently. Everywhere we look society is condoning and encouraging us to have it all right now and pay for it later in "easy, convenient monthly payments." If you've ever been in debt, you know those payments are never easy and anything but convenient.

If you find yourself in debt, don't take the attitude that so many in your situation take, especially at holiday time: "We're so far gone now, what difference will it make if we add on to the credit cards?" Please, believe me: it will make a difference—a big difference. Because when the holidays are past and you've done it without incurring new debt, you're going to be in a perfect position to reverse your current situation. That's a little secret I'm saving for you at the end of this book: I'm going to help you get out of debt completely. So, whatever you do now, don't make things worse.

While every situation is different, the bottom line is the same: *Debt removes options and keeps its prisoners in financial bondage.*

There's no doubt about it. Debt can really ruin your holidays—and your life. And in this country, credit card companies have put such a spin on the matter, they've succeeded quite well in convincing us that, not only is debt good for us, we simply cannot live without it.

To that I say *nonsense.* Just watch us.

Part II
CHRISTMAS BY CHOICE, NOT BY CHANCE

It has always seemed to me the most difficult of problems to combine in daily life are the two parts of the Christian motto; because the effort to show goodwill toward men is only too apt to destroy the peace, and to make home an uncomfortable place where several overworked people sleep, eat and discuss plans. . . . Surely home life would be happier and philanthropy more helpful if we would but let peace . . . rule in our hearts and learn that rest is not selfishness and bustling overwork no true service.

From an essay in the December 1891 *Ladies' Home Journal*

Chapter 4
It's a Matter of Values

Have I mentioned my mail? I get a lot of it because I regularly invite people to write and tell me what's going on in their lives. While it's impossible to respond to every writer, I read all of my mail and am particularly moved by post-holiday letters that invariably read:

> *It's like I spend weeks and weeks going through the motions, making everything as perfect as possible, and all I get is a dark cloud that follows me around right through New Year's Day. I hate to admit it, but Christmas is the worst time of the year for me.*
>
> *No matter how hard I work or how much money we spend, it's never enough. Someone is always disappointed, and it's usually me.*
>
> *My wife works so hard, and I really want to understand what all the fussing and hyperactivity*

*is supposed to prove, but when all the smoke
clears, all I see is a big pile of new bills. What's
the point?*

*I just can't explain it, but something always
seems to be missing.*

*How can we get our kids to stop focusing on
themselves so much? Their Christmas lists go on
for pages and pages. I want them to know and
experience the real meaning of Christmas, but
then I wonder if I even know what that is.*

How could the holidays possibly lack depth and meaning when we do everything right to orchestrate the biggest
social event of the family's entire year? How on earth could
we end up only partly satisfied when we do all of our
favorite Christmas things, decorate to the hilt, shop with all
those neat plastic resources, and entertain the people we
love and appreciate?

Each of us is born with a remarkable mind, a complex
body, and an eternal soul. Your mind has been nourished
and stimulated since the moment you first opened your
eyes to a stimulating world full of things to learn about.
You've been feeding your body on a fairly regular basis
since the day of your birth. And your soul? It longs be filled
with the Spirit of God—the only one who can satisfy the
longing soul. Since Christmas has a fundamental religious

significance for most people, neglecting to nourish our souls results in a vague kind of emptiness—that lukewarm kind of feeling that something isn't quite right. All of that shopping, decorating, and entertaining stimulates your mind and body, but what are you doing to nourish your soul in all of that?

I'm not saying that if you find less than complete joy and happiness at Christmastime you are spiritually bankrupt, only that you've not consciously chosen to have a value-centered holiday. I can say it no better than Jo Robinson and Jean Coppock Staeheli in their delightful book *Unplug the Christmas Machine:*[3]

A lot of people go through the holiday season without a clear sense of what they value. While they have planned the details of their celebrations right down to the kind of cranberry sauce to serve at Christmas dinner, they haven't stopped to ask themselves the all-important question: Why am I celebrating Christmas? They rely on habit, other people's priorities, commercial pressures, or random events to determine the quality of their celebrations. But this is rarely successful.

People need to make conscious choices because Christmas offers them so many possibilities. It's a time to celebrate the birth of Christ, the pleasures of family life, the importance of friendship, the delight of creating a beautiful home environment, the need for world peace, the desire to be charitable and a host of other important values. When people don't sort out which of these ideas is most important to them, the celebration can seem fractured and superficial.

I know you have the ability to successfully produce and direct the Christmas holidays in your home. You've done it efficiently for many years—you can get a lot done in a short amount of time. You know how to do whatever it takes to get through the season and then deal with the consequences later.

On the surface, being efficient sounds terrific and exactly what all of us should be, especially during the action-packed holiday season, right? Well, only if you consider that *more* and *faster* are necessarily better.

If the holidays for you have become a marathon of crossing tasks off a "to-do list" and counting the days until it's over, then I suppose operating efficiently is a worthy goal. But if you're longing for a meaningful time of spiritual renewal and joyful interaction with your family, it is *effectiveness* you should seek.

This brings us to your next assignment: Make a list of the values that guide your life and your family, thinking of them in light of Christmas. Be prepared for this to be more difficult than you might at first think. The following values are very important in our family and are offered here as stimulators to help you get started with your own list.

Responsibility: Being accountable for choosing right from wrong without pressure from a superior authority or guidance. Responsibility means doing the right thing and making the right choices because that is the right thing to do. I believe some people are just born more naturally responsible than others. Some of us have to work harder at it than others.

Trust: Relying confidently on the integrity, honesty, and justice of another without carefully investigating first. To trust means to place one's faith in another person or entity.

Self-control: Being able to motivate and manage one's self, one's time, and one's assets. Self-control means pulling away from the laziness of doing too little and pulling in from the excesses of trying to do or to have too much.

Balance: Paying equal attention to mind, body, and soul; taking into account the mental, physical, and spiritual lives of ourselves and our families. It is the absence of extremes and involves weighing decisions and actions carefully to avoid going off on tangents.

Respect: Caring about how other people feel and demonstrating that care by being polite, courteous, and helpful.

Forgiveness: Ceasing to blame or feel resentment toward another person or situation.

Fairness: Acting in accordance with rules and principles; responding to people and situations with justice.

Honesty: Not lying, cheating, or stealing; acting out of truthfulness, sincerity, and fairness.

Kindness: Being gentle and good-hearted to others; showing compassion and caring; being selfless.

Love: Having a deep devotion or affection for another person.

Now, take a few minutes to think about what stirs your soul at Christmastime. Is it the glorious music that lifts your soul to heaven, the warmth you feel way down deep inside when you give a gift to a child who might otherwise not receive something at Christmas? (If you've never done this, you can only imagine how wonderful it is.) Is it snuggling up with one of your kids in front of the fire and reading *A Christmas Carol*? Is it sitting in a candle-lit Christmas Eve service with your entire family? What is it that really stirs your soul? If your celebrations of Christmas in the past have had little purpose for you other than to do what everyone expects and just get it over with, consider that it's not because you are a bad person or even a person without a value system. It's probably because you've never sat down and thought about how you would complete this sentence:

Christmas is a time to . . .

Here are only a few of the ways you could finish this sentence:

- ◈ spend time with our friends and relatives.
- ◈ show compassion to others who are less fortunate than us.
- ◈ eat and drink glorious foods we don't have at other times of the year.
- ◈ make amends to those we've hurt.
- ◈ exchange gifts with friends or family.
- ◈ send photographs and a family newsletter sharing our joys of the past year.
- ◈ celebrate the birth of Jesus Christ.
- ◈ renew our spiritual commitment to God.
- ◈ relax and rest.
- ◈ give away more than we receive.
- ◈ spend only a predetermined amount of money.
- ◈ make strategic plans for the New Year.

As you consider why and how you wish to celebrate Christmas, remember, there are no right or wrong answers. This is simply an exercise to help you take back control of what happens in your life and in the life of your family during the month of December.

Once you are clear about your values and the specific and meaningful ways you choose to express them, you will have laid a firm foundation for a soul-satisfying celebration.

Chapter 5
Shape Your Attitudes

If your spending habits have caused you to incur holiday debt in the past, you can change the behaviors. You can experience a joyful season without mortgaging your future to pay for a transitory good feeling. You can become a fully committed "no-new-debt, no-way, no-how" kind of person. It's all a matter of attitude—something over which you have tremendous control.

Your attitude is your state of mind, your opinions, your behavior on some particular subject. In this case, the subject is spending money that has not yet been earned. Attitude can be shaped by both feelings and facts.

While you can't change many aspects of Christmas, you can control your attitude. You can also change the things that cause you stress by changing the way you view them.

It may seem completely ridiculous to think that just by changing your attitude you can change your circumstance—but it's true. Disadvantages can be turned into advantages simply by the way you look at them. Think of it this way: one of your freedoms as a human is to choose your attitude in any given set of circumstances. It has been said that the happiest people don't necessarily *have* the best of everything, they just *make* the best of everything.

Here is a life principle that will help you understand and make meaningful attitude changes: *It's easier to act your way into a feeling than to feel your way into an action (attitude).* If you change your attitudes not because you feel like it but because you know that it is the right thing to do, your feelings will follow. On the other hand, if you wait until you "feel like it," meaningful change may be delayed indefinitely. Changing attitudes is a proactive proposition, and sometimes it can be hard work.

It's dangerous to allow your life to be guided by feelings. Feelings are fickle—they cannot be trusted. Not only is it foolish to make choices and decisions by the "if it feels good, do it" method, it can be costly.

Everything about Christmas stimulates our feelings. The music moves our spirits and souls. The displays of grandeur take our breath away. The lights (reflections of the Christ child, whose birth brings peace in the midst of chaos), the gifts, the giving, the children, the snow, the parties and the pageants, the holly and the mistletoe—all nudge us to act emotionally, without much thought about the consequences.

And, of course, while we'd like to, it's difficult to ignore the negative feelings—the worry, stress, and disappointment; the fear of not doing everything well enough; the envy of those who do more and do it better; and the guilt of not measuring up or not giving the right gift or spending enough to even the score.

Christmas can be one overwhelming feeling after another. If we allow our spending to be controlled by our feelings, we're in for a roller-coaster ride with a heavy price tag. It costs a lot of money to satisfy our feelings because they are insatiable.

I'm not for a moment suggesting that we should shut down our emotions during the month of December—or anytime. It's just that our feelings should not direct our lives. That's the job of our values, ethics, and morals.

The key to gaining control over the emotional roller coaster of the holidays is in consciously making intellectual decisions and determining our attitudes in anticipation of the season. It's in recognizing that our heads and our hearts have different roles, and while both are equally important, they shouldn't be confused. It is amazing how quickly the negative feelings of stress, worry, and inadequacy dissipate once we bring our intellects into the decision-making process.

Rather than allowing your attitudes about Christmas and debt to be shaped by your ever-changing feelings brought on by sights, sounds, smells, shopping malls, magazines, neighbors, friends, and family, you can choose to shape your attitudes in a reasoned and logical manner. This is how you can take control of your holiday spending.

I hope that by now you are already thinking about your new attitudes toward the holidays. Start writing your thoughts down so you can focus on them and decide exactly what, for instance, your attitude about holiday debt is. If you're having a tough time getting started, here are a few examples.

Positive Holiday Attitudes

"There are no Christmas laws, rules, or regulations that I must obey." Have you ever wondered who's in control of your Christmas, anyway? Which credit card determines where you can purchase gifts? Perhaps it's time to rethink your attitudes about who's in charge of your holiday actions and activities.

"I won't be buying things that I cannot pay for at the time of purchase because I don't spend money that is yet unearned." This is not a politically correct attitude these days. With some retailers doing the bulk of their entire year's business during the single month of December, they are bent on extending as much credit as possible. Retail marketing as an industry has done such a number on us, it almost seems un-American to not shop with credit cards. It takes a lot of fortitude and determination to make this resolution stick.

Give it time to sink in. Before long you'll find it to be a very freeing attitude that will open your heart and mind to all kinds of creativity and alternative thinking when it comes to gift-giving and bringing joy into your life and the lives of those you love.

"I will determine my holiday spending limits." Determine not to allow credit lines, other's expectations, or your own guilt to determine what you will spend, do, and give. This means that not only will you not spend money you do not have, but that you don't have to spend all the money you do have. It's OK to have cash left over on December 26. Being broke is a lousy feeling whether it is a result of over-gifting or some other financially foolish act.

"No matter what pressure I encounter or expectation I face, there isn't any person or situation that can make me use credit to pay for any aspect of Christmas." And it helps to leave the credit cards at home, at least for the holiday season. Keep this in mind at all times because it will be tempting to give in "just this once."

"Giving a gift is only one of the many ways I can express my love, and I'm willing to consider all kinds of alternatives." Oops. Is this starting to get into uncomfortable territory? If you've been used to buying expensive gifts, the idea of alternative gifts (you'll learn what I mean by this in chapter 9) might be more than you want to consider. After all, we don't want to appear cheap or stingy (which is one of

the attitudes that landed us in holiday debt in the past). But I'm not asking you to reduce your personal standards of dignity or style, only to find ways to express those personal qualities in ways that won't force you into debt.

"I will examine my holiday activities in light of my values, and because there's no way I can do it all, I will choose those things that bring the greatest joy and happiness to me and my family." This must be the best new attitude of all because it offers a big sigh of relief. It's permission to relax and enjoy!

"I am not a Christmas magician, so I am realistic about what I want and what I will do to create a holiday season that gives me and my family the greatest satisfaction." That sure takes a lot of the pressure off, doesn't it? For me and my family, the holidays are a time to rest, relax, and reflect. Plan to do lots of all three. Sounds more like a vacation than the old way of celebrating, doesn't it? Isn't this new attitude thing starting to look better and better all the time?

There. Lots of positive holiday attitudes that have to do with spending. Perhaps they don't fit your value system at all. That's OK—come up with a list of your own. Once you have determined what your attitudes will be, begin to reflect on them. Taking back control of your Christmas holidays by making important attitude adjustments is a wonderful gift you can give yourself.

However, anytime you make changes in the way you've always done things before, expect to feel some resistance. That resistance might come from your spouse, children, friends, or even from yourself. You need to learn how to respond to resistance in a way that will put it to rest immediately.

Attitude Busters

"If I don't use credit cards, I won't be able to buy very nice gifts." The quality of a gift does not necessarily equal its price tag. Gifts from the heart are worth their weight in gold because they touch another's heart. There are many ways to create a gift that costs very little in terms of money. A lack of cash should not eliminate your ability to give gifts, as you will learn in chapter 9.

"Everyone depends on me to put together a spectacular Christmas. I can't do that without money, and I can't disappoint my family." It's a lot of pressure to be the Christmas magician. I'd like to help you find ways to have an even more meaningful Christmas than you ever had before, without all the pressure and stress. You can have a wonderful holiday without outspending your means and without going into debt to do so. This year expect everyone to pitch in. That will free your time and allow all of you to experience a kind of Christmas that doesn't leave one person in the family exhausted and totally burned out on December 26.

Shape Your Attitudes

"My kids are used to getting expensive gifts, and we've always purchased them on credit. I don't know what we'd do if we had to pay with cash." Think about what you've done in the past. You've purchased the gift first and paid for it later. Somehow you've come up with that $75, $100, or more monthly payment every month after Christmas. Right? Why can you afford to pay that much toward Christmas gifts after Christmas, but there's no way you could do it before Christmas? Imagine if you set those payment amounts aside in a savings account ahead of time, what a careful shopper you would be.

Paying with plastic doesn't seem real, somehow. Handing a clerk a Visa card to pay for a $149 CD player doesn't seem the same as handing her fifteen ten-dollar bills. That's the problem with credit. It's too easy and it doesn't seem real. We feel for a moment that we're getting something for nothing, that we're pulling a fast one. Think about how credit card debt has affected your life the other eleven months of the year. Is it really worth it? Do you really think your children's lives would be destroyed if you scaled down a bit this year?

Many parents find it a challenge to create a simple, value-centered Christmas in the midst of all the commercial pressure. But the task is made much easier when they keep in mind the four things that children really want for Christmas. While children may be quick to tell their parents that what they want is designer clothes, the latest electronic gear, and brand-name toys, underneath what they really want are

- a relaxed and loving time with family,
- realistic expectations about gifts,
- an evenly paced holiday season, and
- reliable family traditions.

"I don't want to have to think about Christmas during the year. One month of insanity is bad enough." If you've been used to paying for Christmas on credit, it's been affecting you in a major way every month, whether you like it or not. So, if you're going to devote any energy to Christmas during the year, why not have it be productive in the form of planning and debt-prevention rather than damage control?

"If I give homemade gifts, everyone is going to think I'm cheap." Is that what you thought when your sister-in-law made you a beautiful afghan for your birthday? Was that your reaction when your son gave you a tin-can vase covered with glued-on macaroni full of construction-paper flowers for Mother's Day? Have you ever received a handmade gift and thought how cheap the giver was? Did you ever resent the fact that a friend or relative wasn't willing to go into debt in order for you to receive an expensive gift? Probably not.

"The thought of recycling anything, including wrapping paper and ribbon, gives me a queasy feeling in my

stomach. I'm just not that way." This is a tough one, and something I really understand. Let me tell you what I've learned. A gracious person with uncommon taste and class retains all of those qualities and abilities whether she's decorating her home with unique materials gathered from nature or expensive stuff bought from Bloomingdale's on credit.

I have a friend, Kathleen (you met her when you read my dedication of this book), who dresses like a million bucks. She's got style. It doesn't matter if her clothes come from a thrift store, consignment shop, or Nordstrom's—it's her style and sense of fashion that make it work, not the amount of money she spends. I have other friends who can create treasures from trash—and with great dignity and style, I might add. I stand in awe of anyone who can take such unassuming materials like brown grocery bags, piles of dryer lint, and a few dabs of house paint and create amazing works of art.

So, when those fickle feelings come over you and make you feel queasy, stand up to them and picture yourself as a smart and creative person who has a clear sense of who she is and what she believes. Who you are is not dependent on the price tag on the clothes you wear or the monetary value of the things you're able to purchase. It's your sense of style, dignity, grace, and thrift that define who you are.

"I'm a generous person, and I love giving a special gift that reflects my feelings and generosity. I'm not a miser. I love to buy beautiful things for others, and I don't

care if they cost a lot." Is going into debt and spending money you've not yet earned an appropriate way to demonstrate care? If you call going into debt an act of generosity, you need to think again. Generosity is shown when you give of yourself and what you have, not what you pretend to have or be. Perhaps what you really desire is love and approval. Perhaps something inside of you insists the more expensive the gift, the more approval and love you might receive. A gift that fits within your means and comes from your heart rather than your line of credit seems like a far better way to demonstrate your fondness for the recipient.

"I don't want the kids to think we're in financial trouble." Is that why you've been running the credit cards up in past years, to impress your kids with a false sense of their parents' wealth? Don't make money the issue. If you were to inherit a million dollars tomorrow, would you spend the entire amount on your kids' Christmas gifts? $250,000? $50,000? $1? There has to be a limit, so gather your thoughts—not your feelings—and set it.

Remember: First you change your attitudes, then you change your life!

Chapter 6

Commit to Cash

Decision time. It's time to make the decision that you will do whatever is necessary in order not to use your credit cards to pay for your holiday expenses. I know how difficult such a cash-only commitment can be. But you can do it; I know you can.

Making a personal commitment not to incur any new debt is key in this whole process of debt-proofing your holidays. At this point you may have no idea how you will do Christmas without credit, and that's OK. The important thing is that you are willing to make the commitment.

Make a Written Commitment

Here's a sample no-debt commitment:

> *I am fully committed not to use credit cards or in any way incur debt to pay for any aspect of my/our Christmas holiday celebrations. I will not be guided by guilt or obligation and will do*

*everything possible to keep all expenses well with-
in the amount of money I/we will plan to spend.*

Here are a few suggestions to make sure your promise sticks:

- *Remove your credit cards from your wallet or
  purse.* Never carry them with you. Put them in a safe-
  deposit box, freeze them in a block of ice, or leave
  them in the safekeeping of a trusted friend or relative. Better yet, cancel all but one of the accounts
  (you'll still be able to pay them off with monthly payments) and get rid of them.

- *Prepare for an emergency.* If you are fearful of
  being caught unprepared in the event of a dire emergency (a great new set of golf clubs for your husband
  is not an emergency), write down the account number of one all-purpose credit card such as a Visa or
  MasterCard and that company's toll-free number and
  keep it in a secret place, such as your address book.
  Now you will have the solution in the event of a true
  emergency because you will be able to call the company for approval.

- *Place your written no-debt commitment in a
  prominent place.* The refrigerator door is a good
  place where the whole family can see it often. If
  you think of your goal in a positive and upbeat
  manner, your children will catch your enthusiasm
  and determination.

You should be very proud of yourself. Perhaps for the first time in your adult life, you'll be able to take the dread out of the holidays.

Stash Some Holiday Cash

Yes, you really can sock away a good deal of cash during the year for your holiday spending. Think of it this way: every day, money is leaking out of your life. What you need to do is adopt a plumber's mind-set—find the leaks, plug them, and divert the cash you've recovered into a safe haven.

Stash the Cash in a Safe Place

- *Start a Christmas Club account.* The money you deposit into one of these specialty savings accounts at a bank won't earn much interest, but that's not the point of your stash. The small weekly deposits won't be missed and will provide you with a sizable check when the holidays roll around.

- *Deposit your holiday funds in a savings account in a bank in another city!* Find an independent bank that will allow you to open an account with a minimal amount of money and won't charge large service fees. You can make all your deposits, large or small, by mail. Once a year at holiday time you can make the drive to pick up the cash or arrange for an electronic transfer to your local bank. This is the best alternative if you are concerned about keeping these funds safe from yourself. If you have your holiday savings in a really convenient place, like the bank up at the corner, you may be tempted to keep borrowing from it.

🎁 *Make a mini-vault.* Clean and dry an empty mayonnaise jar, being careful to leave the labels intact. Carefully spray or brush the inside of the jar with white paint. Allow to dry, and you now have a perfect little vault for your holiday stash. Store in the back of the refrigerator.

How to Fund the Stash

🎁 *Don't spend coins.* Make a new rule for yourself and any other family members you can convince to participate: Do not spend coins. If your tab comes to $4.03, hand the clerk $5 and get excited about 97 cents of beautiful change. Every evening, empty the coins in your pockets and wallet into a change jar. When it accumulates, roll the coins and get them into your savings account. My husband, Harold, taught me this trick years ago, and we are still amazed by how much we're able to sock away by simply not spending coins.

🎁 *Stash coupon savings and refund proceeds.* When you receive a refund or rebate for the purchase of a product at the supermarket or through the mail, don't spend it. Stash it in your special fund. At the grocery store have all of your purchases subtotaled and write your check for this amount. Now, have the checker reduce the total by your qualified coupons and receive those savings back in cash. (Most grocery stores allow a customer with proper identification to write a check for more than the purchase.) Make sure you don't commingle the savings, and then rush the amount—no matter how small—into your stash.

🎁 *Rethink a regular habit.* We all have a few spending habits that could either be cut back or eliminated with little lasting impact on our lives. Perhaps, for you, it's that large coffee you purchase every morning or those two daily sodas you buy from the vending machine. You don't have to eliminate these altogether, just think them through, make some cost-cutting adjustments, and consciously put the savings into your holiday stash on a regular basis. Instead of purchasing soda one-can-at-a-time from the vending machine, buy a case at the warehouse club and bring your own to the office. Stash the difference in price between the 75-cents-a-can variety and the 20-cents-a-can version. Instead of purchasing that coffee from the vendor, get a small

coffeemaker for your desk. I'll bet that in a month
you'll have saved enough to pay for the pot, the
cup, and enough coffee to last for six months or
longer. Do you really have to eat lunch out every
day? Cut it back to two days, brown bag the other
three, and stash the money you don't spend on the
food that passes so quickly through your life!

- *Do it yourself.* Consider how much money you
  could save if you stopped paying someone else to
  perform tasks you and your family members could
  do: lawn maintenance, housekeeping, washing the
  cars, etc.

- *Crash save.* Decide that for, say, a few weeks you
  will not grocery shop for anything other than milk
  and fresh produce (or whatever strict guidelines fit
  your particular lifestyle). I'm not advocating you and
  your family take up fasting, but rather that you use
  up all of the food you have in the pantry and freezer.
  You probably have a huge investment in canned
  goods and other perfectly good items that just sit
  there. You will be amazed at the creative meals you'll
  come up with. And the money you don't spend on
  groceries for those weeks can go into the stash.

- *Save your "extra" paychecks.* If you're paid biweekly
  (every two weeks), in two months of the year you will
  receive three paychecks. The months vary according

to each year's calendar and the day of the week on which you are paid. Stop right now and plot that on the calendar. Anticipate those months, and when you receive those two checks—you guessed it: straight into the stash.

- *Stash expense account reimbursement checks.* Many people are required to travel as part of their job or use their own funds in other ways and are then reimbursed by the company. If this is your situation, stretch yourself to pay most or all of the expense out of your regular income. When you receive the reimbursement checks, don't even think about spending them. Instead, add the money to your holiday stash pile.

- *Adjust tax withholding.* This is delicate, so hear me out. If you routinely receive a refund when you file your income taxes this means you are having too much money withheld from your earnings by your employer. You are in essence giving the federal government an interest-free loan. You send in way too much money, tell them to keep what they need, and send you a refund after the first of the following year. That doesn't make too much sense to me. If this is your situation, consider changing your withholding by filling out a new form with your employer and adjusting the number of exemptions on your claim so that your withholding will more closely resemble the amount of tax you owe. A perfect adjustment would mean you neither owe money nor receive a refund when you file your taxes next year. The result of such an adjustment to your withholding will be a fatter paycheck. But don't get used to the new amount. Arrange to have the difference automatically deposited to your stash.

Bring a little moonlight to your life. Think about volunteering to work overtime once in a while, get an occasional weekend job, pick up a little money baby-sitting—anything to attract small amounts of cash. Do this with the sole purpose of funding your stash. We're talking about money that would only evaporate if you added it to your normal income, but little dabs here and tiny bits there will definitely add up in your stash.

Chapter 7

Develop a Plan

You probably wouldn't add a family room to your home without a blueprint, make a new dress without a pattern, or head off on a cross-country vacation without a map. But when it comes to preparing for the holidays, most of us hit the ground running the day after Thanksgiving—without blueprint, pattern, or map. We get caught up in all the emotion of the season, and before we know it, we're taking Christmas three stairs at a time.

Oh, I know you probably have a gift list—all of us have one of those, and it gives the illusion of a plan—but, believe me, that's not it.

Make a Written Plan

If you wince at the thought of approaching this holiday season with a written plan, afraid that it will turn spontaneity into rigidity, think about the alternative—debt is the result of reacting compulsively. The more of Christmas you leave to chance, the greater the potential debt load you will carry into the next year.

Please don't resist the idea of making a plan, no matter how threatening or uncomfortable it might feel at first. Remember: don't trust your feelings. Once you and your family have decided what you want from the celebration of Christmas, you'll be able to make adjustments and corrections as the season unfolds and even treat yourselves to some deliciously spontaneous times along the way.

State Your Purpose

Your holiday plan should start with a purpose statement describing what you and your family want the holidays to "look" like. Simply write a sentence or two summarizing your ideal Christmas, making sure this reflects those values you identified in chapter 4 and the attitudes you adopted in chapter 5. Remember: there are no rules, no correct or incorrect responses. This is the way to tame the monster that used to come barreling through your lives every December.

Use the Calendar

Your holiday blueprint should be built around your calendar. It will assist you in managing your time and your holiday spending plan, which will help you manage your resources. Flip back to chapter 2 and review your responses to the queries about how you would have changed things in holidays past. Now is the time to make corrections, so that you never lose control again.

Plan According to Your Values

Consider holding a family meeting to create your family's "Top Five Holiday Values." Take nominations from each member of the family, and once you've decided on a final list, write them down and post them where everyone can see them. Values might include enjoying the family, experiencing an old-fashioned simple Christmas, strengthening personal relationships, exchanging only gifts that cannot be purchased in stores, celebrating Christ's birth, eating glorious creations from the kitchen, attending musical performances, decorating the house, directing the school pageant, singing in the community choir, relaxing-resting-recuperating, reaching out to those who are less fortunate, visiting relatives and entertaining friends, and so on.

Next, ask questions, such as in what specific ways can our values be expressed in our homes and lives during the Christmas season? How can we share our blessings with other people?

If, for instance, one of your top five values is "Christmas is a time to spend more quality time as a family," how specifically will you do that? And when? If you decide that everyone will play hooky from work and school one day to do nothing but sleep in, play Monopoly, put together a jigsaw puzzle, and bake Christmas cookies (which, by the way, I think is the best idea I've had in a long time), then decide right now when that will be. Mark out the whole day on the calendar so nothing will interfere.

Or if one of your values is "Christmas is a time to exchange gifts with friends and family," answer specifically who, what, when, and how much? Wow! This is a lot of work, huh? Not really. Consider it a trade-off. Either you do the work now in a relaxed and reasoned way or you'll have to do it the old way—on the fly and without much control.

Continue through your values list and watch as the calendar fills up. Keep in mind that many activities will come up to fill your holidays—activities that may not be included in your list. Address those issues now. Which activities will you decline? Which parties will you attend? What about the office parties and activities? Which days will you leave unscheduled to allow for free time? Which days will you devote to gift-making, shopping, and wrapping?

Develop a Holiday Spending Plan

It is vital that your holiday planning include a specific and detailed spending plan, designating the overall amount you plan to spend and how you plan to spend it.

To start, make a chart that will allow you to visualize your spending categories, such as gifts for kids, spouse, grandparents, other relatives, friends, service givers, coworkers, and employees; gift wrapping; Christmas cards; postage; photo session; baking ingredients; tree and home decorations; admission for holiday events; baby-sitting and travel costs; charitable donations; new clothes; etc.

In a column with the heading "$ Amount Plan," write down the amount of money you plan to spend on each category.

Total all of the categories to see how much cash you will need for your expected holiday expenses. Whoa. It's probably a lot more dough that you anticipated or even have available at the moment.

Did you ever dream your holiday expenses were so huge? No wonder Christmas has sent you to the credit cards in the past. Likely, your list will need scaling down, and now is the time to do it.

I hope you've used a pencil because you'll need to do a lot of erasing and refiguring. First, erase the total and write instead the total cash amount you intend to have available to spend for the holidays. You may have to resharpen that pencil often before you get your expected spending to match your total available cash.

If the list is really out of balance—your expenses clearly outweigh your available cash—start whittling down that enormous gift list. Many times we feel compelled to give a gift when a nice card, photo of the kids, and a personal note would convey the intended goodwill. Go through your list with this in mind, and put a star next to those who will be getting cards as gifts this year.

If you still have a discrepancy, there are two things you can do: reduce expenses even further or find ways to come up with more cash.

In the chapters that follow, I'll be giving you lots of ideas for low-cost and no-cost ways you can achieve your holiday expectations. A lack of cash should not eliminate your ability to give gifts.

The Envelope System

Once you have a good spending plan in which your estimated expenses and available cash are on speaking terms, get a stack of envelopes and label one for each of your holiday-spending categories. Place the amount of cash you intend to spend in each category in the corresponding envelope and put the envelopes away in a safe place.

When you go shopping, leave the credit cards at home and take the appropriate envelopes instead. It will be easy for you to keep track of expenses because you'll know precisely the moment you are finished spending—when the envelope is empty.

Fringe Benefits of Cash-Spending

If you have been accustomed to paying for holiday shopping with credit cards, or even a checkbook, the all-cash method is going to feel very strange in the beginning. Expect to feel timid and fearful that you might run out of funds. You may find yourself hesitant to spend "that much" of the available cash on a single gift. (Isn't it funny how a check or credit card doesn't feel as real as actual cash?) Actually, these are helpful responses because they will make you think more carefully about your purchases. Cash-spending will also compel you to find the best bargain.

When shopping with a limited amount of cash, you will be less prone to spend compulsively. You will become a disciplined consumer, and your entire holiday outlook will change.

Chapter 8
It's Never
Too Early

There are many things you can do throughout the year that will require very little in terms of time or thought and little, if any, money, but these tiny efforts will multiply come Christmas.

Drying Plant Material

Purchasing dried flowers at holiday time can be very expensive. But during the year whenever you pick wild flowers, receive gifts of flowers, or make cuttings from your own yard, if you handle them properly, you will have all kinds of wonderful material for holiday projects. If every season you are on the lookout for ways that you can recycle nature's bounty, you will have wonderful decorations for Christmas packages, wreaths, garlands, and centerpieces.

Designate a place in your home where you can gather and store dried material. I have a large box in a closet, which I can get to easily and where everything stays dry.

In principle all plant material can be dried. Selecting the proper method is the key.

Drying by pressing. Flowers that are delicate, with thin petals and leaves, can be dried between sheets of absorbent paper inserted between the pages of a thick book. In two or three weeks the book's weight presses out the flowers' moisture, which is absorbed by the paper. Pressed flowers combined with a ribbon and bow adorning a brown-kraft-paper-wrapped gift makes a very elegant package suitable for shipping.

Drying by hanging. Flowers like roses, hydrangeas, yarrow, baby's breath, heather, statice, and larkspur can be air-dried simply by tying them in bunches and hanging them upside down in a dark, cool, dry place where air can circulate around them.

Herbs that dry well this way include English pennyroyal, lavender, wild thyme, and rosemary. Simply divide the herbs into small bunches, hang them in a well-ventilated spot, and allow to dry for about ten days. Gently wrap them in tissue paper and put them away until December. If you aren't up to growing your own herbs, buy them in season at farmer's markets, grocery stores, and gourmet shops.

Drying by desiccants. Desiccants are moisture-absorbing substances such as sand, silica gel, borax, and yellow cornmeal. Silica gel, available at garden shops, drugstores, craft shops, and floral supply stores, is by far the best because it is lightweight and won't damage the flowers, and it can be used over and over again. (Silica gel isn't really a gel at all. It resembles granulated sugar.) With silica gel the drying process generally takes one to two weeks, compared to three weeks or more with sand.

Fill a jar halfway with silica gel. Gently insert a piece of florist wire into each flower. Stand the flower upright and gently pour in enough crystals to cover all the petals. Seal the container for at least two weeks.

Drying in the microwave. The latest and fastest way to dry flowers is with the microwave method. The heat of the microwave evaporates the moisture in the flower or leaf and this moisture is then absorbed by the silica gel.

You'll need a microwavable container or cardboard box with a tight fitting lid. Layer about one inch of silica gel into the bottom of the container. Place the flowers or leaves on top of this layer leaving about an inch between the container's side and between individual flowers. Add another one-inch layer of silica gel on top.

Place your uncovered container in the microwave. If you're using a cardboard box, elevate it on a microwavable drain rack so the moisture can escape through the bottom of the box.

If your microwave has settings from 2 to 10, put it on setting 4 (about 300 watts); a microwave with 3 or 4 settings should be put on "half" (about 350 watts); and a microwave with a "high" and "defrost" setting should be set on "defrost" (about 200 watts). Because microwave ovens vary, you'll need to experiment with the "cooking" times. The drying time for one to five flowers with leaves in about one-half pound of silica gel is roughly 2 to 2½ minutes.

Remove the container from the microwave oven, cover the container tightly, and allow to stand for up to 30 minutes. Then empty the box or dish onto a newspaper and gently remove the flowers.

Reusing silica gel. This stuff is so cool. When totally dry it is blue. As the granules start to absorb moisture, they turn whitish-pink. So just keep checking the color, and when you know they've reached full capacity, you can turn them back to blue. Preheat your conventional oven to 300 degrees. Spread a single layer of silica gel evenly on the bottom of a shallow pan and place it uncovered in the oven. Stir the granules every once in a while and watch them turn blue. Allow to cool and immediately place the silica gel into an air-tight container.

Holiday Combining

Think about how many holidays share the colors and symbols that can be incorporated into Christmas: Valentine's Day offers hearts of every size and material, red candies, red paper goods and wrapping paper, red and white candles.

St. Patrick's day brings an array of everything in the color green: green candles, green paper goods, green ribbon and papers. Easter brings out loads of baskets and big plastic eggs that can be used for unusual and unique gift presentations. Thanksgiving is the time to pick up gourds, small pumpkins, and all the other really cheap accessories that can be spray-painted to include in wreaths, garlands, and gift wrapping. Make sure you're thinking Christmas as you check out those day-after-the-holiday, near-giveaway prices.

Vacations

What better time to pick up all kinds of things you'll be able to use at Christmas than when you're away from your usual surroundings? Seashells make wonderful additions to packages, wreaths, and garlands. Museum gift shops often offer very low-cost and unusual items that will make wonderful gifts or decorative items. You're not under pressure here; just keep your eyes open and your brain in gear!

Thrift Shops and Flea Markets

As you happen on to these events during the year, watch out for small pieces of antique lace, doilies, buttons, buckles, fabric trim, ribbons, old books with charming illustrations, etc. Use them to make a gorgeous Victorian tree, wreath, or garland. Framed pages from old children's books can be a wonderful gift for a new baby's nursery.

Old Toys

Anything vintage of the toy or stuffed animal nature can make wonderful nostalgic displays in your home at Christmastime.

Miscellaneous

There are many things you can collect during the year in order to take the pressure off the month of December: Mason jars, unusual glass containers, and narrow-necked bottles to contain gifts from the kitchen; brown grocery bags or shopping bags to wrap gifts; white bakery bags and candles to make luminaries; mailing tubes and paper towel and toilet tissue rolls to make unusual gift wrapping or party favors; shirt cardboard and the tops from frozen juice containers to make ornaments; corks to make stamps.

The craft market is booming. There are hundreds of books on crafts, from the most complex to the simplest projects for kids—and everything in between. Check out the possibilities in your local library. I'll also give you ideas about how to use the materials creatively in the following chapters. You'll find dozens of unique uses for those dried roses, pieces of cardboard, old corks, and seashells.

Part III
ANTI-DEBT HOLIDAY SOLUTIONS

Chapter 9
Gift Ideas

In this country we've become a bit brainwashed into
believing that proper Christmas shopping must take place in
a shopping mall. The problem with malls is all the behind-the-
scenes action designed to lure you into spending like there's
no tomorrow.

From the moment you drive into the parking lot,
Christmas is in your face in the form of wonderful smells
from the bakeries, gorgeous decorations, choirs serenading,
and jolly Santas ho-ho-ho-ing; and it's really tough to keep
your mind on the task at hand. I say visit the malls, but not
for the purpose of shopping. Buy a cookie, give a buck to a
sidewalk Santa, and wander about in a soak-it-up mode. But
when it comes to spending your holiday cash wisely—according to your holiday spending plan—you'll be surprised how
much further your money will stretch when you stay out of
the mall.

Mall Alternatives

- *Art-supply stores* for stationery items (mine sells lovely writing papers and matching envelopes by the sheet and also by the ounce or pound), imported brushes ideal for makeup, fine writing instruments at reasonable prices, photo albums, and all kinds of wonderful portfolios. Chalk, crayons, pads, modeling clay, and packets of construction paper make terrific gifts for kids who will always be attracted to the simple things.

- *Office supply stores* for memo books, calendars, pens, and pencils. An appreciated gift for anyone would be a nice box with lid (or any other kind of unique container, even a wastebasket) full of those items you need around the house, but can never seem to locate: colored paper clips, staples, tape, labels, writes-on-anything pen (Sharpie is the best), coin wrappers, index cards, Post-it notes, or any combination thereof. Great idea: Yellow pads or any kind of writing paper and a personalized rubber stamp. Rubber stamps are fairly cheap and can be ordered from an office supply store.

- *Hardware/home-improvement stores* for all kinds of gadgets and widgets. For the home chef try an eighteen-inch length of 1⅞-inch wooden dowel for a professional-style rolling pin, a large unglazed terra cotta tile for a pizza/baking stone, or a new 1½-inch paintbrush for a pastry brush. A collection of screws, cup hooks, small tools, etc., can all be packed in a small tool box for the homeowner. Stroll the aisles, and you'll get all kinds of great ideas including unusual wrapping materials such as wire and painter's tape. Let your mind wander. You'll be quite a hit.

Here are some other alternative shopping locations you may want to try:

- Military surplus outlet
- Marine supply store
- Garden center
- Health food store
- Damaged-freight outlet
- Restaurant supply store
- Antique store
- Museum and gallery gift shops

Gifts of Food

It's hard to go wrong by giving a delicious, consumable gift. Breads, cakes, cookies, herbed vinegars, flavored mustards, jams, jellies, chutney, and pickles are just a few of the food items that make appreciated holiday gifts. Most popular, however, is homemade candy.

Here are several recipes for homemade candies that

store and travel well but, best of all, are economical and easy to make.

English Toffee

2 cups sliced almonds, 2 cups milk chocolate chips,
1 cup butter, chilled and cut into bits
1½ cups light brown sugar, firmly packed

Preheat oven to 325 degrees. Spread almonds on baking sheet and toast in preheated oven, stirring occasionally until lightly browned (about 5 minutes). Allow to cool (and I mean very cool—even cold—so that the nuts do not melt the chocolate). Chop the chocolate chips by hand or in a food processor, pulsing on and off until they are coarse. Transfer to a medium-sized mixing bowl. In the same processor bowl, coarsely chop the toasted almonds. Add to chocolate chips. Toss to combine. Spread half of mixture evenly over bottom of a well-greased 13-by-9-inch baking pan. In a heavy medium saucepan, bring butter and brown sugar to a boil, stirring constantly over medium heat. Cook 5 to 7 minutes, or until syrup is light golden-brown and just reaches the hard-crack stage (300 degrees on a candy thermometer). At that point, a bit of syrup when dropped into a bowl of ice water should separate into hard, brittle threads. Pour hot syrup evenly over nut mixture. Top with remaining nut mixture, smoothing and pressing down gently with a spatula. Refrigerate until toffee is set and chocolate is firm, about 1½ hours. Cut into squares or break into irregular shaped pieces. Store in a tightly covered container in refrigerator up to two weeks. *Yield: 20 large pieces.*

Holiday Fudge

Combine in a large mixing bowl and set aside:
6-ounce package semi-sweet chocolate chips,
1 cup chopped walnuts, 1 teaspoon vanilla,
½ cup (1 stick) butter or margarine.

Combine in a saucepan:
12 large marshmallows, 2 cups granulated sugar,
1 6-ounce can evaporated milk.

Bring ingredients in saucepan to a boil, stirring constantly. Boil exactly 6 minutes (time this carefully) and remove from stove. Immediately pour this hot mixture over ingredients in the bowl. Stir to combine and then beat by hand for exactly 20 minutes. Pour into a lightly buttered 8-inch square glass dish. Sprinkle a few ground nuts on top and refrigerate to harden. Cut into squares. *Yield: 40-45 pieces.*

Cinnamon Munch

⅓ cup granulated white sugar,
1¼ teaspoons cinnamon,
¼ cup (4 tablespoons) butter or margarine,
4 cups Corn Chex, Rice Chex,
or Crispix cereal or 3 cups Bran or Wheat Chex

Mix sugar and cinnamon and set aside. Melt butter/margarine in large skillet. Add cereal and mix well. Heat over medium heat, stirring until coated (5 to 6 minutes). Sprinkle ½ of the sugar mixture over the cereal and continue stirring until well coated. Sprinkle with remaining sugar mixture and heat several more minutes. Spread on a layer of paper towels to cool. *Yield: 3 to 4 cups.* This recipe multiplies well if you have a large enough skillet.

Mulled Cider

In a large pot steep 1 gallon of fresh apple cider with ¼ cup brown sugar, 12 whole cloves, 8 allspice berries, and 6 split cinnamon sticks over very low heat for 20 minutes. Ladle into mugs. Garnish each serving with a cinnamon stick. *Yield: 6 cups.*

Hints for Giving Food

- A single recipe can be divided into several gifts. Simply arrange pieces of fudge or toffee on a pretty Christmas plate (paper is fine) and wrap in clear cellophane topped off with a pretty ribbon or embellishment.

- Snack foods can be presented in a small tin or Chinese take-out container. If you don't tell, no one will have to know just how easy and inexpensive these delicious gifts really are.

- Write down a favorite family dessert recipe and place it along with all the required ingredients in an appropriate new baking or serving dish. Wrap everything and top with a big bow.

- Present your edibles in special containers: an interesting bottle, a nostalgic candy box, a pretty jar.

- Fill a nice or comical mug with flavored coffee, tea, or hot chocolate mix. Wrap it along with a devotional book.

- Fill a cookie jar with home-baked cookies. Include the recipe.

- Wrap up the ingredients and recipe for mulled cider. (see page 84 for the recipe.)

- Give your own Cookie-of-the-Month (or Quarter for the less ambitious): Bake one dozen to include in the holiday gift, along with a card announcing your recipient will receive another dozen each month all year long. This can be one of those gifts that's easy to give but more difficult when it comes to following through, so give cautiously.

- Even if you don't cook or bake, you can still give wonderful, inexpensive gifts of food. Buy quantities of nuts, fancy cookies, fresh coffee blends, candies, or dried fruits. Repackage these into those small, unique containers you've been collecting all year.

- A simple mug or teacup and saucer (either antique or new) can be a wonderful gift when filled with special candies. Wrap in a piece of clear cellophane gathered at the top and tied with a lavish bow.

- A simple cookie cutter in a holiday shape of a star, tree, or gingerbread man can make a great little gift. Lay the cookie cutter in the middle of a piece of clear cellophane. Fill the center of the cookie cutter with tiny candies such as jelly beans. Gather the cellophane and wrap with a bow.

- Personalize your food gift with your own label: Millie's Chutney or Minerva's Cookies sound very special.

- Attach your recipe to the gift with ribbon, piece of raffia, or a tasseled cord. Add a spoon or spreader for chutneys or flavored butters.

🎁 Present candy in bags or boxes your children have decorated with drawings or stick-on decals.

Gift Ideas for Adults

🎁 Foolproof recipes are always welcome gifts. Make a pretty little notebook and copy (by hand or photocopy) twenty of your favorite recipes. Add a personal note, if you like.

🎁 Set aside two hours a week to serve as chauffeur, escort, or errand runner for a special person who doesn't drive or doesn't have time to get to the library, grocery store, pharmacy, dry cleaners, post office, etc.

🎁 Offer to keep children of young parents overnight once a month or once a quarter. Arrange to pick them up in mid-afternoon so the parents can prepare for the evening together.

🎁 Offer to care for a pet during a vacation.

🎁 Give a Dinner-a-Month to an overworked mom. Offer a piping hot and ready-to-eat casserole once a month. She can specify her busiest evening.

🎁 Force bulbs so you can give a beautiful in-full-bloom plant of paperwhites. Directions for forcing them to bloom: Fill a shallow container with rocks or decorative pebbles and add water until it reaches just below the surface. Set the bulbs on the gravel and add more pebbles to hold them upright. Set the container next to a window away from direct heat. As the leaves appear, rotate the container so the bulbs will grow evenly. The flowers will bloom in four to six weeks and will last two weeks at room temperature. (The bulbs cannot be repotted.)

- Make a beautiful watering can for a plant or garden lover on your gift list. Either buy a new watering can or give an old one a face-lift. You'll need some self-adhesive shelf liner or covering and a pair of scissors. Cut the covering into a strip to wrap around the handle, another for the water spout, then larger pieces for the can itself. Peel away the backing and carefully wrap the can completely. The end result: a functional watering can that's pretty enough to be used as a vase.

- Make a collage or memory box for a person who made that "special trip" with you. Arrange postcards, ticket stubs, foreign currency, luggage tags, airline boarding passes, and street maps and combine with photos of the trip.

- Fill a blue basket with a variety of blueberry products such as jam, muffin and pancake mix, syrup, blueberry-scented candle, bath salts, room freshener, and blue note paper. The same idea can be used for strawberry, lavender, peppermint, or other flavored variations.

Gift Ideas

🎁 To turn a plain cookie sheet into a fancy bistro tray, glue on canceled foreign stamps and/or domestic commemorative stamps. Cover the entire tray, then apply several coats of polyurethane varnish.

🎁 To make a calendar with special meaning for a family member, start with a fun wall calendar from your local bank or other business. Select twelve family photos, preferably ones commemorating such special occasions as birthdays, a christening, or a wedding. Make a color photocopy of each photo, the same size as the illustrations on the calendar. Paste the photos on the month in which the pictured occasion took place. Your local copy center may also offer this service.

🎁 Everyone has a box or two of old family photographs. For a special vintage touch, choose a black-and-white one that has a special meaning for the recipient. You can frame it in its original form or have a photocopy enlargement made at the copy store. An inexpensive black or silver frame will turn this treasure into an heirloom.

🎁 Buy or make calendars and write birthdays, anniversaries, and other important dates in them. They make great gifts.

🎁 Give a working woman's emergency kit: a small Swiss Army knife; a good lint roller (a pet-hair remover from a pet store is the best bargain); an assortment of safety pins, needles, and thread; Kiwi's Shine Wipes (instant shoeshines); double-stick tape to fix hems in a hurry; small scissors; a glue stick (better than clear nail polish for arresting a hosiery run); antistatic spray; several pencil erasers (the tiny eraser end from a pencil makes a dandy temporary replacement for the back piece of a pierced earring). Put everything in a small, compact container such as a pretty box or fabric bag.

- Offer an evening of baby-sitting to someone who cannot afford a baby-sitter.
- Go to a magazine stand and select a magazine you know someone would enjoy, maybe because of a hobby or a secret desire—to sail or skydive, for example. Wrap up the current copy of the magazine with a note saying, "Look forward to this all next year!" Be sure to mail in the subscription card with a check.
- A wicker bed tray or other container with fixings for breakfast in bed—muffin mix, jams or jellies, coffee beans, plus a subscription to the *New York Times*.
- Books make great gifts. But don't limit yourself to shopping in the big chains. Secondhand bookstores are less expensive and often have out-of-print titles that can't be found elsewhere. Also, these stores

may sell old prints or maps that would reflect personal interests and be suitable for framing.

🎁 Pass along an heirloom to the next generation. Write up the story of the piece and encourage the recipient to display, use, and enjoy this new treasure.

🎁 Make an appointment for a beauty makeover for a young mother (haircut, facial, and manicure) at a local beauty college. Volunteer to take care of the kids.

🎁 Gather old family movies, take them to a camera shop, and have them transferred to videotape.

🎁 Share a cord of firewood with a neighbor. Announce the gift in a card tucked between several logs wrapped with a wide ribbon. If possible, stack the wood between your properties.

🎁 A videotape makes a very special holiday greeting or gift. Put together a video with highlights of the past year. You might include birthday celebrations, summer vacation footage, sporting events, a school play, and other special moments from throughout the year. A festive way to end the tape might be to gather the family and sing "We Wish You a Merry Christmas." A tape like this will bring joy to faraway family members long after Christmas has come and gone.

IOU: A Great Gift

Custom-designed gift coupons are a wonderful way you can give of yourself, your time, and your talents, which are, of course, more valuable than money, and often more difficult to part with. But before you haul off and agree to more than you're able to deliver, think carefully. A good coupon says you know what the receiver really loves or really needs. Give what you love to do, or this gift will become more of a burden than a blessing. Here are a few suggestions that could follow that standard opener, "This coupon redeemable by bearer for":

- Two hours of silver-polishing.
- Six one-hour computer lessons. (Great for a dad to give a child.)
- The making and delivery of a dessert the next time you have company (24-hour notice, please).
- One pair of mittens—you pick the yarn.
- One complete car wash, wax, and complete cleaning inside and out.
- Total care and appropriate spoiling of your children for a complete weekend so you can get away. Ample notice requested.
- Offer an I'll-Teach-for-a-Day coupon to a home-school mom to give her a day off. Center your day's lessons around your special talent or expertise.

Gift Ideas for Teenagers

- Create Night-on-the-Town certificates for fast-food, a movie, and the ice cream shop. This is a gift a teen will love.
- Make an appointment for a beauty makeover at a local beauty college. Prices are typically very inexpensive and all work done by students is highly supervised. Stick with temporary work such as hairstyling, manicure, pedicure, and facial and stay away from haircuts, perms, and hair-coloring.
- Calligraphy pen and instruction book.
- An address book with names, phone numbers, addresses, birthdays, and anniversary dates of family and friends.
- With parental permission, a pretty drawstring pouch for the soon-to-be-teen filled with lip gloss, clear nail polish, bubble bath, dusting powder, and light scent.

Gift Ideas for Kids

- Books as well as books-on-tape are always welcome gifts for kids of all ages. Ask your librarian or an elementary school teacher for recommendations.
- A personalized Book-of-the-Month. Either write and design the book yourself or buy an inexpensive one that reflects the appropriate holiday or season.

🎁 For a young girl who loves to play "dress-up," cover a shoe box with pretty wrapping paper inside and out. Fill it with inexpensive makeup and costume jewelry.

🎁 An old suitcase filled with old "dress-up" clothes such as shawls, dresses, hats of all kinds, veils, pocketbooks, high-heeled shoes, etc.

🎁 A homemade balance beam with proper supports for an aspiring gymnast. Make sure you start with sturdy material and sand and finish the surface very smoothly.

🎁 An appliance box, with doors and windows cut out and decorated to look like a house, castle, office, or school. This idea is in accordance with the rule that says the bigger and more expensive the toy, the more likely the child will want to play with the box it came in.

🎁 Piggy bank with starter money.

🎁 Homemade play dough. Combine the following ingredients in a saucepan: 1 cup flour, ½ cup salt, 1 cup water, 1 tablespoon vegetable oil, 2 teaspoons cream of tartar, food coloring. Mix and cook over medium heat, stirring constantly, until a ball is formed. Pour onto a floured board or wax paper and knead until smooth. Tightly covered, it will keep for several weeks.

🎁 A simplified map of the town in which the child lives. Highlight the location of significant landmarks:

child's school, church, Daddy's and Mommy's offices, the zoo, and the library.

🎁 A birdhouse with a supply of birdseed.

🎁 Kids love to create little books with "coupons" in them for their siblings, good for things like one night's dishwashing or a kiss and hug. Parents can give reverse coupons to their kids also—good for exemptions from making their bed, setting the table, or such.

🎁 Tickets to a favorite sporting event or for a ride on a real train (accompanied by an adult, of course).

🎁 Embroidery piece, thread, needles, and hoop and certificate for lessons from the giver.

🎁 Simple camera, film, and photo album.

🎁 Magazine subscription. *Brio* and *Breakaway* are excellent magazines for teen girls and boys, respectively; also *Clubhouse* is a magazine for children ages 8 to 12 and *Clubhouse Jr.* for ages 4 to 8. Call Focus on the Family at 800-A-FAMILY for more information to subscribe to these magazines.

🎁 A one-of-a-kind puzzle. Mount an enlarged photo of yourself or some family occasion onto a piece of foam board (available at stationery or art supply stores). Cover the photo with a piece of tracing paper and lightly draw a jigsaw pattern, making as many or as few pieces as would be appropriate for the age of the recipient. Using a sharp knife (like an X-Acto), carefully cut through the tissue paper, photo, and board along the puzzle lines. Separate the pieces and place in a gift box.

- Preschooler puzzle. Lay a strip of masking tape on a table, sticky side up. Press about ten popsicle sticks (or wooden tongue depressors) side by side, evenly across the tape. Draw a picture and write the child's name on the sticks. Then remove the tape and shuffle the sticks to make a great puzzle.

- For an artist's box, start with a clear storage box (12-quart is a good size). Write the child's name on it and fill it with plain white paper, construction paper, crayons, colored pencils, paste, tape, a ruler, plastic stencils, and a pencil sharpener.

- If parents say yes, give a kitten or puppy from the local Humane Society. Wrap up all the necessary equipment, such as a food dish, litter box and litter, toy, collar, and food.

- A collection of Christmas tree ornaments for a child and add to it every year.

- A beginner stamp-collector kit from the post office for children. They are very inexpensive and geared toward the young philatelist.

Gift Ideas for Senior Citizens

🎁 An adult child can give Date-a-Month coupons to a parent. A man setting aside time to spend alone with his mother, or an adult daughter taking her dad out once a month is a lovely gesture. Some months your evening together might include a movie; other times, just dinner and time to talk and listen.

🎁 Donate your services as chauffeur to an otherwise homebound elderly person, or offer to do their food or gift shopping for them.

🎁 Take Grandma or Grandpa on a "movie date" at their house. Rent a video or borrow one from the library. Take along drinks and popcorn. Great gift for a teen to give.

🎁 Give a book-on-tape to a senior citizen whose eyes are failing. Wrap with a small headset and tape recorder. Lend them your tapes and offer to drive them to the library for more.

🎁 A subscription to the large-print edition of the *New York Times* is a wonderful idea for an older person with vision problems. This comes out weekly and provides a summary of the week's news. A six-month subscription is $35.10; an entire year, $70.20 as of this writing. To order, call 800-631-2580 or write to the *New York Times,*

Mail Subscriptions, P.O. Box 9564, Uniondale, NY 11556-9564.

- Fill a pretty box with a variety of different occasion greeting cards, a pen, and a roll of stamps for someone who is housebound.

- A photo album for grandparents filled with pictures of baby's typical day—morning bath, breakfast, taking a walk, playing, greeting Daddy, being rocked to sleep. Update photos throughout the year as baby grows and the days are more eventful. A video tape with baby as star is also a terrific gift.

Gift Ideas for College Students

- Send a Christmas basket to a college student on the first of December. Include holiday cassette or CD, decorations for the dorm room, Christmas cards, stamps, red and green pens.

- Make or purchase an oversized laundry bag with the recipient's name (great for a college student or single) on the front. Fill with detergent, fabric softener, bleach, and a roll of quarters. Add a couple of magazines for the laundromat wait.

Whole Family Gifts

To cut back on the number of gifts you buy, consider giving one gift to the whole family at Christmas and save individual presents for birthdays. The challenge, of course, is to make sure the gift appeals to each member of the family. First, think about what the family cares most about as a family. Are they campers? Sports-minded? Perhaps this is a more literary family that spends a lot of time at the library. Here are some whole-family gift suggestions:

- A newspaper subscription from the family's old hometown.
- Two decks of cards and a book of card games.
- The hottest new board game on the market.
- A 1000-piece jigsaw puzzle.
- Croquet set.
- Badminton set.
- Gift certificate to a local pizza parlor.
- Subscription to a magazine that reflects the family's interests, such as travel or skiing, or a magazine like *National Geographic, Smithsonian,* or *Air and Space.*
- Food dehydrator.
- Ice-cream maker.
- Binoculars.
- Charitable donation made in the name of the family.
- Video movie.
- Computer game.
- Bird feeder and supply of birdseed.

Gift Baskets

A basket filled with delicious treats and fun gadgets will please just about anyone on your gift list if it's tailor-made. Choose an attractive container—it doesn't have to be a basket—decorate and fill it. Your "basket" can be as simple or as extravagant, as big or as small, as your budget and imagination allow.

A gift basket can be a terrific gift for the entire family, including the family pet. The basket itself can actually cost less than fancy wrapping paper. Be on the lookout all through the year at garage sales, secondhand stores, and craft stores.

Prepare the Container

Some baskets require no preparation and are perfect just the way they are. But if you want to do something even more special, or refurbish a basket that's looking a bit tired, you'll need spray paint, a glue gun, and appropriate embellishments such as silk or dried flowers, raffia, lace, or ribbon. Chances are you already have lots of appropriate decorating materials around the house.

Of course you can use any kind of basket, but a pottery bowl, copper colander, oversized coffee cup and saucer, lightweight platter, cloth shopping bag, novelty-shaped cake pan, plastic salad spinner, metal bucket, baking rack, small baking sheet, flower pot, or teapot will make your gift basket even more unique.

Fill the Basket

Once you start thinking creatively you won't have to worry about where to start, but rather where to stop. As you fill the basket, lean items at an angle rather than stacking everything vertically. Presentation is most important.

Holiday Basket Ideas

Here are a few basket suggestions to get your creative juices flowing:

- **Bath basket:** Bubble bath, lotion, bath powder, fragrance, scented candle, back brush, loofah sponge, soap, book, cassette tape of relaxing music.
- **Gourmet's basket:** Fresh herbs tied in a bundle, fresh spices, unique kitchen tools, recipe cards, jars of gourmet mustards and salsas.
- **Artist's basket:** Brushes, brush cleaner, sketch pad, palette, beret, sponges, small canvas, colored pencils.
- **Picnic basket:** tablecloth, napkins, plastic plates, utensils, candleholders, candles, salt and pepper shakers, plastic bags, bug spray.
- **Letter writer's basket:** An assortment of greeting cards, stamped postcards, stationery, postage stamps, pens, pencils, return address labels, a small calendar with clever notations of significant dates.
- **Mother of a preschooler basket:** Activities (books and games) for the kids, coping manuals, babysitting

coupons for a night or weekend away from it all, bubble bath, romantic novel.

🎁 **Pizza basket:** Checkered napkins, pizza stone, recipes, special flour, spices, jar of pizza sauce, cheese, pizza cutter.

🎁 **Gardener's basket:** Work gloves, trowel, seed-marking stakes, seeds or bulbs, decorative pots, sun bonnet, tiny birdhouse, sunscreen.

🎁 **Breakfast basket:** Homemade jelly, pancake mix, muffin mix, biscuit cutter, honey, cinnamon sugar, mugs, gourmet coffee, crepe pan, favorite recipes, tea.

🎁 **Christmas gift-wrap basket:** Curling ribbon, wrapping paper, gift bags, tissue paper, gift enclosure cards, transparent tape, scissors.

🎁 **Coffee lover's basket:** Bag of exotic coffee beans, coffee mug, ½ dozen bagels, a bagel cutter.

🎁 **Family night basket:** Popcorn, video, deck of cards, puzzle, candy.

General Gift Principles to Consider

🎁 When you give someone a gift you've made yourself, you give of yourself. Big or small, a handmade gift is a personal expression of caring. A homemade gift shows you care enough for that person to make him or her something original and special.

Gift Ideas

🎁 Try going in together with others on gifts. Sharing the cost will reduce, by at least half, the price of a gift.

🎁 Some gifts should be considered token gifts and, as such, should be small enough and of a low enough value that the receiver doesn't feel obligated to reciprocate.

🎁 The value of a gift is not necessarily equal to its price tag. There are many gifts you can give that cost absolutely nothing in terms of money.

🎁 It is not up to you to find the exactly perfect gift that will fulfill the deepest heart's desire of your recipient. It's not your responsibility to become the ultimate mind reader and desire fulfiller. A gift is simply an expression of your fondness for the recipient.

Chapter 10
Cards and Gift Wrapping

If you need to cut back on the cost of the holidays, gift wrapping is a great place to start. In fact, depending on the supplies you already have available, there's a very good chance you can get through the season without purchasing any gift-wrapping materials. Here are some gift-wrapping tips:

- Set up a gift-wrapping area. Drape a card table with a large tablecloth or sheet that hangs to the floor. Hide wrapping supplies under the table for quick retrieval.

- Tie a couple of pieces of a child's favorite candy (wrapped in colored plastic wrap) to the outside of a gift.

- Sew little pouches of red or green velvet, put small gifts inside, and tie with a holiday ribbon.

- Outsmart kids who are prone to snooping by wrapping gifts before you hide them. Instead of using tags, put a color-coded self-stick dot on each package so only you know who it's for.

- Don't throw those wrinkled gift bows away. You can reuse them by placing the bows in the dryer along with a damp washcloth. Set the machine on "fluff" cycle for two minutes. The bows will come out looking like new.

- Turn ordinary shoe boxes into colorful gift boxes. Use an X-Acto knife to cut simple designs like stars on the sides and top of the box. Paint the box with brightly colored acrylic paint. Wrap the gift in tissue paper of a contrasting color and let it show through the cutouts.

- Brown paper is not just for mailing packages. Dressed up with stickers, doilies, fancy ribbon, and such, it's a wonderfully inexpensive way to wrap gifts. You can either purchase kraft paper in a roll, or recycle brown grocery bags. Cut them open and lightly iron them on the nonprinted side. (A very light misting with spray starch will help iron stubborn wrinkles and folds away.)

- Instead of buying expensive holiday wrapping paper, purchase a large roll of white butcher paper and a bolt of red plaid ribbon from a florist supply store.

- Don't buy gift wrap. Start saving the comics from the Sunday papers in the summer, and by Christmas you'll have a good supply. You can also use foreign newspapers or fashion ads.

🎁 Make a "Santa Sack" for each of your children, or all members of the family for that matter. Sew together two large panels of Christmas fabric (approximately one yard each) on three sides, add a drawstring to the top and then attach a name tag. Drop in the gifts from Santa, and place the sack under the tree. You can explain that the elves are much too tired to wrap after making all those toys. These Santa Sacks can be reused every year, which will create a new family tradition.

🎁 If you use a plain-colored box, wrap only the lid. It saves paper and makes the gift easier to open. If the box is not plain, wrap the box and lid separately. It's easier to open and allows the box to be reused.

🎁 Find paper that's appropriate for the gift or recipient. For example, wrap a cookbook with pages from a beautiful food magazine or use sheet music for a music-lover's package.

🎁 To remove creases from folded or wrinkled wrapping paper, lightly press them out with your iron, set on the lowest setting. Don't steam the paper. For persistent wrinkles, spray the wrong side lightly with spray starch. (Ironing not recommended for waxed or foil papers.)

Cards and Gift Wrapping

🎁 Save your kids' drawings and use them to wrap gifts. Tape several together if the package is large. This will be a big hit with grandparents especially.

🎁 Visit a decorator fabric shop, upholstery supply store, or sewing supply store and look for braids, cordings, tiebacks, fringes, and tassels to use instead of ribbon. Bolt ends are often sold as remnants at just a fraction of their retail price.

🎁 Use new, colored, or patterned shoelaces to tie up small packages. Add jingle bells for that special touch.

🎁 Snip sponges into fun shapes, then dab in poster paint and press in a decorative pattern on the insides of those brown paper grocery bags that you've cut open. This also works well for decorating cards and invitations.

🎁 Wrap odd-shaped packages in handkerchiefs.

🎁 Wrap a gift for a traveler in a road map.

🎁 Cut two matching tree shapes out of felt to cover a tall bottle, such as herbed vinegar or maple syrup. Sew or glue the sides together, leaving the bottom open, then cut out felt ornaments and glue them onto the tree.

🎁 Wrap a gift in plain white paper and decorate with curved shapes cut from red, yellow, and blue scraps of construction paper, or other colored paper. Use a glue stick to attach them.

- Place a gift box diagonally on a square scarf and tie opposite corners together at the top. Tie again with gold cord or ribbon.
- Wrap a box in brown paper, then hot-glue rows of pennies to the outside in a symmetrical design, randomly, or in the shape of a Christmas tree. Tie with a copper-colored or white ribbon.
- If the gift is really large, don't waste yards and yards of pricey paper. Just spray-paint the carton and add a bow.
- A car, or even a bicycle, can be "wrapped" by tying an oversized gift tag to a piece of string. Leave the tag under the tree and run the string to where the gift awaits.
- If the gift is just too cumbersome to wrap at all, or didn't show up in time for Christmas, or didn't quite get finished, wrap a smaller box containing some kind of clue about the gift to come, plus a claim check for redeeming it.
- Instead of racing out to buy all sorts of mailing materials, try recycling things you have around the house. Cut a brown paper bag to accommodate the item you're sending. Using heavy tape, seal around three of the sides. Slip the gift into the mailer and tape up the fourth side.
- Use those cardboard tubes from gift wrap or paper towels as mailing tubes. Simply cut them

to the desired length and seal the ends with strapping tape.

🎁 A coupon-clipping tool works beautifully to cut wrapping paper quickly.

🎁 If the paper doesn't quite fit the package, try laying the item diagonally so the corners can be folded toward the center.

🎁 Use a glue stick instead of tape when you wrap. It's invisible and much easier to work with.

🎁 If time is short or gift wrapping is especially difficult, use a white plastic garbage bag (two, if they are too transparent) tied with a great big bow. With presents, as with people, it's what's inside that counts!

🎁 Turn silver-lined potato chip bags inside out, wash, and use as gift bags. Tie with pretty ribbon.

🎁 Recycle the silver-lined mylar potato chip and popcorn bags into gift ribbon. Wipe the empty bag with a damp cloth to remove all traces of salt and oil. With scissors, cut one long "ribbon" of your desired width starting at the top and spiraling around the bag. Curl as you would regular curling ribbon.

🎁 You can purchase pastel and brightly colored paper lunch bags at a discount store very cheaply. Decorate and use for gift bags. Wrap gift in tissue and place in bag. Fold top of bag down and punch two holes through all thicknesses. Thread a ribbon through the holes, then tie a bow or add curly ribbon.

🎁 Cut strips of wrapping paper and curl it with the edge of a scissors blade the same way you would curling ribbon. This requires a gentle touch so the paper ribbon does not tear, but the final effect is really nice.

Prepare for Shipping

🎁 When you need to pad a package, recycle wherever possible. Instead of bubble wrap and Styrofoam, use newspaper. If someone you know has a paper shredder, ask for a bagful of shreddings. You can also use the edges of computer paper. Use stale, air-popped—not buttered—popcorn and include a note instructing the recipients to keep the gift and give the popcorn to the birds.

🎁 Cut empty wrapping-paper tubes to fit a box you are mailing. They cushion the contents but add little weight.

🎁 Don't use shoe boxes for mailing because they tend to split.

🎁 Surround dishes, glassware, and other fragile items with plastic air pillows by filling zip-type plastic bags with air and sealing.

🎁 If you use Styrofoam "peanuts" as a packing cushion, spritz them with an antistatic spray first.

🎁 The U.S. Postal Service says address labels should be legible from thirty inches away. That's about an arm's length.

🎁 Mark packages that contain breakables as "Fragile" in three different places: above the address, below the postage, and on the reverse side.

🎁 Use filament-reinforced tape to seal packages for shipping. Do not use twine, string, or cord—they will get caught in the automation equipment.

🎁 As you unwrap gifts this year, save discarded paper, ribbon, and packing material to use as packing material next year.

🎁 Enclose a piece of paper inside the box on which you've written the address of the recipient and yours as the return.

🎁 Just before you seal up a box for mailing, sprinkle in some pine-scented potpourri. When the carton is opened, the whole room will smell like Christmas.

🎁 If you write the address directly on the box, use a waterproof marker.

🎁 Mail early!

Gift Tags and Christmas Cards

🎁 Don't buy gift tags. There are so many ways you can use materials you already have to make unique, clever, and quick gift tags.

🎁 Recycle old Christmas cards to make gift tags. Cut out a part of the design, punch a hole, and tie it on.

🎁 Call or stop by a local print shop and ask for any scraps of colored paper they are discarding. Around the holidays you'll end up with lots of green and red scraps. Cut the green paper in the shape of holly leaves, add tiny red berries cut from the red scraps and you have beautiful gift tags. Make blue stars and yellow bells. The possibilities are endless.

🎁 Using holiday-shaped cookie cutters as a pattern, cut tags from file folders or other heavy card stock. Decorate with stickers, markers, or rubber stamps.

🎁 Instead of writing the recipient's name on the tag, attach a childhood photo. It's fun for the kids to try to match the grown-ups with the pictures.

🎁 Get a marking pen that writes on glossy surfaces like gift wrap (Sharpie is a popular brand; check stationery and art-supply stores), and you can skip the gift tags entirely.

🎁 Just in case the tag falls off packages under the tree or while in transit, write the name of the recipient on the back of the wrapped gift.

🎁 Make your own stamps with Christmas symbols for hand-decorated cards and gift tags. Draw a pattern on the wide end of a cork. With an X-Acto knife or some similar sharp implement, carefully cut the cork away from the design to a depth of about a quarter of an inch. Stamp cork onto a stamp pad and press down hard on the paper. Because corks are small, so are the images, therefore plan to make lots of different simple shapes like hearts, stars, and trees.

- Send postcards instead of traditional Christmas cards. They are cheaper to mail and can be made by the clever sender by recycling last year's cards.

- Once the season is over, don't throw out the cards you received. If you don't plan to use them yourself to make postcards or gift tags, send them to St. Jude's Ranch for Children, a residence for abused children at 100 St. Jude Street, Boulder City, NV 89005. The kids at St. Jude's make new cards out of your old ones and sell the cards to support the ranch. For more information or to place an order for cards call 702-293-3131.

- If you have a very long Christmas card list and feel rushed to write the personal notes you love so much, divide your list over four or five holidays such as Valentine's Day, Easter, Halloween, Thanksgiving, and Christmas. Explain that this is your annual greeting. To keep your records straight, color code every name in your address book to denote on which holiday you wrote the note.

Chapter 11
Decorating Your Home

Isn't it wonderful the way our eyes become mercifully selective once our homes are dressed for the holidays? The slightly worn carpet and tired sofa seem to disappear when upstaged by even the simplest decorations. Likely you already have more than enough materials in your drawers, attic, and yard to turn your home into a warm and attractive setting for holiday celebration. What you need are some great idea starters.

- Candles are a simple and natural way to decorate for Christmas. If all you have are pine-tree greenery and candles, you have all you need. Use candles lavishly and light them as often as possible. Nothing will turn your home into a softer, more beautiful place faster than candles.

- Line your walkways, drive, or other areas on your property with luminarias made from paper bags filled with two inches of sand with a votive candle in the center.

- To make punched-tin luminarias that can be kept from year to year: Rinse out an opened tin can and pinch all rough edges flat and smooth. Fill the can with water and freeze. When the ice is solid, remove from the freezer. Using a permanent marker, draw designs around the sides of the can, making sure the design does not come within one inch of the bottom. Place the can on its side on a towel so it won't slip. With a nail and hammer, punch holes along the design lines you've drawn. Leave about a half inch or so between each punch. Then allow the ice to melt and drain. Place a votive candle in each can and line your sidewalk. Light your luminarias every night during the holidays.

- Decoupage a serving tray with last year's Christmas cards (they're probably sitting somewhere in a drawer), and set on your coffee table.

- Make golden angels by gluing silk-leaf wings and a hazelnut head to a pinecone, then spraying with metallic paint. If you don't have silk leaves, cut leaf shapes from cardboard.

- For an instant table dress-up, heap shiny Christmas balls of all sizes in an elegant glass bowl. Place near candles and allow the light to bounce off all the shiny surfaces of the centerpiece.

DEBT-PROOF YOUR HOLIDAYS

- Wrap a tinsel garland around the bedroom or bathroom mirror.
- Arrange poinsettias in a bare corner and tie big, bright bows around the pots.
- Instead of decorating the outside of your home to please your kids, decorate each child's room and get them excited about the holidays. Help your children make red and green paper chains from construction paper to hang all over the room. Not only is this activity less time-consuming than attempting a big exterior display, it may also establish a special tradition your children will not forget. Plus you won't have to say "time for bed!" twice when your child can nestle amongst the enchanting lights of her very own bedside boughs.
- Wrap your child's bedroom door with gift paper to transform it into a giant package.
- Put white twinkle lights on your large houseplants.
- Hang mistletoe in every single door of your house.
- Frosted fruits are a delicious-looking centerpiece and are simple to make. Simmer apple jelly with a little water, let cool, then brush over fruit. Roll in granulated sugar to coat.
- Put Christmas lights and a small wreath on the dog's house.
- Gold, one of the gifts the wise men carried to Bethlehem, is a symbol of generosity. For a truly

glittering Christmas, recycle miniature pumpkins and squash from Halloween and Thanksgiving by spraying them with gold paint. Place them throughout the house or use in centerpieces, garlands, and topiaries. Gild walnuts, pinecones, bay leaves, dried flowers, apples, pomegranates, pineapples, lemons, and grapes. Wear gloves, a dust mask, and glasses or goggles when spraying.

- For just the price of wrapping paper and ribbon you can decorate your entire home in a truly spectacular way. Gift wrap all of the framed paintings on your walls. The effect is stunning. Tip: Wrap only the fronts and sides, and you'll use less paper.

- Decorate the guest bath by wrapping a tissue box like a gift.

- Sew small brass jingle bells along the hem of a tablecloth.

- Increase the effectiveness of votive candles by placing them on squares of mirrored glass.

- Make it a personal creative challenge to decorate with only those things you already have in the home.

- Lay sprays of evergreens on the mantelpiece, thread a string of white lights (on green wire) through them, and nestle some of your collectibles or Christmas balls amidst the greens. If you have no evergreens in your yard, find a friend or neighbor who would allow you to trim some of theirs.

🎁 Cover the mantel or a wide windowsill with a bed of Spanish moss. Tuck in ivy, holly, pinecones, and a few gilded nuts and fruit.

🎁 Pile red apples on a bed of evergreen and tuck in some tiny Christmas balls.

🎁 Drape a long rope of greens (tied together with narrow-gauge wire) over the front door. Attach a red velvet or satin bow in the middle and weave matching ribbon through the garland like a streamer. As a finishing touch, place a poinsettia plant on each side of the doorway.

🎁 Hang your holiday wreath on a four-inch-wide silk ribbon right on a mirror in your entryway or over the mantelpiece.

🎁 Fill a basket with large pinecones interspersed with clusters of delicate baby's breath, then thread tiny white lights throughout, hiding the wires under the pinecones.

🎁 Hang extra mirrors around the house during the holidays to add to the glow and to multiply the special effects of your decorations.

🎁 Wind strands of tiny white Christmas lights and greens around and up the banister. Add large plaid bows.

Decorating Your Home

🎁 Place a poinsettia or flowering plant on every step of a staircase to peek through the banister.

🎁 Tape, tie, or staple Christmas cards to ribbon streamers to hang for display.

🎁 Put several different sizes of poinsettia plants in cache pots or baskets and add trailing ivy.

🎁 If the kids' rooms, basement, or spare rooms are always messy, just shut the doors and hang wreaths on them.

🎁 Fill a glass container with holiday candy and top with a lid or a circle of gift wrap or foil. Tie with ribbon and set on a table.

🎁 Decorate doors with Christmas trees cut from white foam-core board. Pin, tape, or glue on bright ornaments and garlands of beads.

🎁 Paint a bright red "bow" on a doormat. Add a painted tag with the family's name.

🎁 Make a gumdrop wreath. Either buy a Styrofoam wreath or cut one out. Use toothpicks or stiff wire to attach red, white, and green gumdrops to the wreath or use multicolored ones to resemble Christmas tree lights. Top the wreath off with a big bow.

🎁 Fill a large glass bowl three-quarters full of water. Place small, flat-bottomed candles such as a tea lights in aluminum foil muffin tin liners and gently set them afloat in the water. Light them carefully and enjoy.

DEBT-PROOF YOUR HOLIDAYS

- Use crystal or cut-glass bowls of different sizes to make a holiday arrangement: Fill one bowl with Christmas balls—either place them upside down to hide the hangers, or tie a small bow on each. (This is a great way to use ornaments that are damaged). In another bowl combine fresh fruit with evergreens. In a third bowl add holiday-scented handmade or purchased potpourri. Place votive candles in the smaller bowls.

- Try a wreath centerpiece. Core five apples, making a two-inch-deep hole at the center of each to hold a candle. Lay a wire wreath frame on a flat surface and attach the evenly spaced cored apples with a glue gun. Arrange cedar, spruce, and holly sprigs in one direction along the wreath and wrap in place with fine wire. Attach small pinecones with a glue gun and insert tall, tapered candles in apples.

- Create a fruit centerpiece by tying individual oranges (lemons, limes, or apples will also work) with ribbon, then stack them into a tree shape on a pedestal plate.

- Set out pretty containers of pine, evergreen, or cinnamon potpourri in every room.

- Keep plenty of throws and afghans around the living room. They look great and invite people to curl up and get cozy.

- Display all your holiday cards so they add to your home's decor. Attach a piece of string that is just a bit

longer than a front window and attach the ends to
either side at the top of the window. "Hang" the
cards from the string by folding them over the string
so the front of the cards face out. Once full, the
string will drape ever so slightly to give a beautiful
valance effect across the top of the window.

🎁 Attach wreaths on the inside, as well as the outside,
of your doors.

🎁 Make pomander balls; it's an easy kids' project. Buy a
supply of whole cloves (they're expensive at the
supermarket; try a health food store that sells spices
in bulk) and some oranges. (Even little fingers can
insert the cloves if you poke holes in the rind first
using a small knitting needle.) Wrap the pomanders
with red ribbon and hang them around the house.

🎁 Rather than buying new decorations, enlist your
kids' help to refurbish old ones. Give life to a wreath
by adding fresh ribbon. Glue glitter on faded ornaments.

🎁 Go back to old standards like popcorn-and-
cranberry garlands and construction-paper chains.

Trimming Your Tree

🎁 Make play clay ornaments. In a saucepan, stir together
2 cups baking soda and 1 cup cornstarch. Add 1¼
cups water. Cook over medium heat, stirring

constantly, until mixture is the consistency of moist mashed potatoes. Turn out on a plate and cover with a damp cloth until cool enough to handle. Roll to ¼-inch thickness. Cut shapes with cookie cutters. Use a drinking straw or toothpick to make holes at the top of each ornament. Allow to dry and harden on flat surface overnight. Paint, decorate, then protect with a shiny glaze.

- Bend medium-gauge wire into the shape of a heart or wreath, then thread with popcorn or cranberries. Top with a bow.

- Decorate a tiny live tree with fruit ornaments and ribbon and set on the kitchen table or countertop.

- Cut out pictures from magazines, greeting cards, or wrapping paper and glue them to circles of construction paper or cardboard. Attach loops of ribbon to ornament backs and hang on the tree.

- Help very young children make Christmas ornaments out of red and green pipe cleaners. Twist them into the shape of candy canes, stars, and trees and hang on the tree or use to decorate packages.

- Cut the bottom out of a plastic berry basket, trim into the shape of a snowflake, coat with glue, and dip into glitter.

- Draw free-form stars and snowflakes in varying sizes on wax paper with white glue that dries hard (like

Elmer's White Glue). Sprinkle with glitter, covering the glue completely. Allow to dry for two days. Then, starting at the points and working in, carefully peel away the wax paper. Hook the stars and snowflakes over the branches of the tree.

🎁 String garlands of cranberries on thin wire or heavy nylon thread or fishing line because the berries can become quite heavy.

🎁 String popcorn garlands with stale popcorn because it's easier to handle.

🎁 Let kids make paper snowflakes out of white or silver paper doilies. Fold each into eighths and cut designs into all three sides of the wedge. Each one will turn out differently. Attach a ribbon loop to the back or just tuck the snowflakes into the tree branches.

🎁 Cover small Styrofoam balls with white glue and attach fresh cranberries. Allow to dry, attach a ribbon, and hang on the tree.

🎁 Make paper ornaments out of cardboard. Trace cookie cutter shapes or draw designs freehand. Color the shapes and cut them out. Punch a hole at the top; pull ribbon or string through the hole.

🎁 Any recipe for crisp, rolled cookies can be used to create cute and edible tree decorations. Simply roll and cut the cookie dough as usual, but before baking, use a drinking straw to make a hole near the top of each cookie. (Repeat if hole closes up during baking.) When cookies have cooled, thread ribbon through the holes.

🎁 You know those plastic, fruit-shaped lemon- and lime-juice squeeze bottles you can get at the grocery store? Save them because they make great tree decorations. Rinse out the containers and let them dry. Thread a six-inch piece of yarn or ribbon through the loop in the lid (or if there is no loop, tie yarn around the cap) and hang on the Christmas tree.

🎁 Create a gift tree. You'll need small boxes of all sizes and shapes (empty Jell-O boxes are perfect), wrapping paper, and coordinating curling ribbon. Depending on the size of your tree, you'll need thirty to fifty small, empty containers. Wrap each with paper and curling. Tie the "gifts" to the tree starting with the small ones at the top and ending with the larger ones toward the bottom. You can use different patterns of wrapping paper or wrap every gift in the same paper and ribbon. This is especially dramatic with gold or silver foil packages and small white lights.

🎁 Thread polystyrene peanuts together as garlands for the tree.

🎁 Save all the toys your kids receive during the year with fast-food meals and use them to decorate a small artificial tree just for them. Tie the toys on with ribbons, but allow them to take the toys off and play with them. This will help make your fancy tree with fragile decorations a little less tempting.

🎁 Place star, tree, or other holiday stickers back to back along a wire or ribbon. Wind these with the garland through the branches of the tree.

🎁 Tie bows all over the tree.

🎁 Instead of a traditional evergreen tree, bring a potted tree in from the garden or terrace for the holidays, or decorate any indoor plant or tree with small ornaments. Small red ribbons on a Norfolk pine, masses of white lights on a ficus, or any plant covered with colorful popcorn and cranberry garlands can be very festive.

General Guidelines

🎁 Attach strings of lights from the bottom up. Concentrate them on the bottom two-thirds of the tree, and then gradually thin them out toward the top.

🎁 Use lots of lights. If your tree is loaded with a mind-boggling collection of different ornaments, limit the lights to one color to help tie everything together. If the tree is sparse, lights in a variety of colors and shapes will help fill things out.

🎁 Attach lights first, garlands next, then ornaments.

- Work from the inside out when hanging ornaments. Put some large, shiny ones on the innermost branches to reflect light and eliminate dark spots.
- To brighten the center of the tree, wrap the trunk with foil or garlands of gold tinsel.
- Hang your most attractive ornaments at eye level on the outermost branches.
- If you don't have a huge collection of ornaments, fill out the tree with Christmas cards, candy canes, ribbons and bows, tinsel, and snowflakes cut from paper doilies. Tiny boxes covered with gift wrap can look surprisingly elegant. Hang gingerbread men, cinnamon sticks tied with bows, and seashells. To add glitter, hang walnuts, pinecones, bay leaves, or blown eggs spray-painted gold or silver.
- Experiment with different tree toppers: a china doll dressed in her Sunday best, a big fluffy gold-lamé bow, a bouquet of dried flowers.
- Don't forget to decorate the base of the tree. A pretty tablecloth; a yard of lace, satin, or silk; an arrangement of potted plants; or even a collection of dolls and stuffed animals can make your tree look unique.
- Know your trees. Balsam and Fraser fir are strong and fragrant and hold their needles well. Scotch and White pine are the most popular and least expensive

trees. They retain needles through the season and have a good scent, but they can't support many dangling ornaments. Spruce trees have sharp needles, but they're good for holding heavy ornaments.

- Test a tree for freshness by running your hand gently over a branch. Needles should bend, but stay on. Pick up the tree and thump the trunk. A few brown needles may fall off, but the green ones should stay on.

- To make your tree sparkle, use lots of miniature lights. To figure out the minimum number you need, multiply the tree's width in feet by eight, then multiply that figure by the tree's height. For example, a four-foot-wide tree that's five feet tall would require 160 lights ($4 \times 8 = 32 \times 5 = 160$).

- Evergreen garlands and wreaths generally last about three weeks. To keep them fresh, mist with water regularly.

- Buy a living tree to use for the holidays and then donate it to a local park or forest once the Christmas season is over. First call your state or local parks and forestry commission to find out where the tree can be planted after the holidays. Other organizations that might enjoy a new tree to add to their landscape are libraries, churches, or schools.

🎁 Many states have designated forest areas where you can chop down your own tree, provided you have secured a proper permit. Other areas have commercial Christmas tree farms where the kids can help choose and cut the tree. (Typically it's no bargain, but when combined with a family outing, it might be worth it).

Outdoors

🎁 If you're fresh out of oversized Santas for the yard and have no snow for snowmen, make a family of "broom people" to warm the hearts of passersby. Stick the broom handles into the lawn. Cut white circles for eyes from felt or white cardboard and draw black dots in the center for the pupils. Glue these "eyes" to the bristle part of the brooms. Top with real hats and ear muffs; tie scarves around the handles. Let your imagination go wild, not your pocketbook.

🎁 Tie outdoor lights to trees and posts with strips cut from the legs of old pantyhose.

🎁 Surround window frames with greens and strings of outdoor lights.

🎁 Hang "tin" ornaments cut from foil pie plates on a tree or bush near the house and watch them sparkle.

Chapter 12
Holiday Entertaining

Inviting friends and family to your home during the holidays doesn't have to end up costing you a fortune. The key to effective entertaining is to remember that your guests are far more interested in spending time with you than seeing you fret and fume as you attempt to pull off the event of the century. So relax, remember what's really important, and enjoy your guests enjoying themselves.

- Use Christmas stickers or fancy stamps to dress up plain notepaper for invitations or thank-you cards.

- When you're hosting a party, arrange the appetizers, snacks, and beverages on several tables. This keeps everybody circulating instead of gathered at the one spot where the food is. You could also ask guests who seem a little shy to pass around appetizers; it helps them break the ice.

DEBT-PROOF YOUR HOLIDAYS

- Make an ice ring for your punch bowl with fruit juice or sherbet instead of water. It looks pretty and it won't water down the punch as it melts.

- Instead of everyone in your circle of friends hosting a separate holiday party, make plans to have a progressive dinner. Start with beverages and hors d'oeuvres at the first house, appetizers or soup at the second, main course at the next, and dessert and coffee at the last. It's an enjoyable way to share the burden—and the glory—and you get to see everyone's holiday decorations too.

- Be realistic about how much you can do. You don't have to see everyone between Thanksgiving and New Year's, for example. Save some get-togethers until after the holidays, and you'll have something to look forward to.

- If you're having two holiday parties or get-togethers at your home, schedule them back-to-back. Serve an identical (or at least similar) menu. It takes the same amount of time to make a double batch. Bonus: All your serving pieces will be out, and your house will be clean.

- Rather than overschedule, host a party the week after Christmas when the house still looks great and you don't feel as rushed.

- Rule: Never serve red punch. It stains carpeting.

Holiday Entertaining

🎁 Try the "Five-Minute Emergency Cleanup for Unexpected Guests." Put all the clutter from the floor and tabletops into a large box or basket. Hide the basket or box. As you circle the room collecting clutter, use a rag to wipe up any crumbs or obvious dust. Pick up newspapers and magazines and neatly stack them on the coffee table. Spray some pine- or cinnamon-scented room freshener. Pick up any towels on the bathroom floor. Hang some; throw the rest in the tub and close the shower curtain. Wipe the sink. Pull out a special basket (prepared ahead of time and stashed under the sink) with a couple of pretty holiday towels and guest soaps tucked in it and place the basket on the vanity. Turn off a few lights (to hide the dust) and sit in the glow of the Christmas tree.

🎁 Next year plan to keep one room sparkling clean just for visitors, and don't let anyone in it before you have guests.

🎁 To cut back on entertaining costs, hold a joint party with a friend or relative and split the labor, as well as the expense. Or have a caroling party and just serve cookies and hot drinks.

🎁 Instead of a full-fledged dinner party, host an adults-only coffee party where each guest contributes a dessert. This way everyone makes something really special, and the emphasis is on being together instead of one person being up to her kneecaps in preparation and hostessing.

- If you have a pretty table, let it show. Make a simple place mat by cutting holiday fabric into a rectangle and ironing on a hem with fusible webbing.

- If you don't have adequate matching flatware and dishes for a large group—most people don't—don't be afraid to mix and match. Just tie everything together with matching napkins.

- Create a simple centerpiece. Trail greens or ivy down the center of the table, then add fresh fruit or holly for color, plus craft-store pearls for sparkle.

- Dress up your napkins by tying each with a ribbon and a small bell.

- Put a small, framed photograph of each person at his or her place instead of traditional place cards.

- Use unusual serving dishes. Put crudités in brightly colored mugs or bread in a shiny metal colander.

- Garnish platters with Christmas colors. Arrange cherry tomatoes and mint leaves, or fresh dill and sliced red peppers, around the edge.

- Display your holiday cookies in a special way. Arrange them on colorful tissue paper or in pretty baskets lined with Christmas fabric.

- Be realistic about the menu. Don't choose recipes that are too elaborate or require last-minute preparation. If you have time only to cook one really blowout course, make it dessert because that's the last impression everyone will take home with them.

🎁 Don't be afraid to use prepared foods. Put a store-bought appetizer on your finest china, garnish it with herbs, and no one will know the difference.

🎁 Do as much work in advance as you can. Bake and freeze desserts and side dishes in microwavable containers.

🎁 Organize your refrigerator for easy access to the food you'll be using most. Put all the appetizer or salad supplies together in a container or on a tray—labeled and ready to use.

🎁 When guests ask to bring something, let them. But be specific about what you need so you don't end up with too many of one thing.

🎁 Set the table the day before with everything (including platters) to make sure it all fits and looks attractive. Cover with a clean sheet to keep dust-free.

🎁 If you are having a large group, consider a buffet. Just be sure to choose dishes that can be served at room temperature and will still look good after sitting out for an hour or so.

🎁 Copy your favorite cookie recipe on a card, wrap colorful cellophane around a couple of freshly baked samples, and tie everything with a bright red ribbon. Give one to each guest as a favor.

- Be prepared for surprise guests and keep some generic gifts (candy or comics for kids, candles or calendars for adults) at the ready. Use color-coded wrap, stickers, or ribbon to help match the gift to the recipient.

Chapter 13
Family Fun

Dream with me awhile. Think about yourself twenty years from now. You're gathered around the table with your children, grandchildren—perhaps even some great-grandchildren. Conversation turns to Christmases past. What will your children tell their kids they loved most about that long-ago Christmas? Seeing Mom spend days on end cleaning the house so Grandma would be impressed? Will they even remember how many gifts they received or even those they gave? Probably not. They'll remember the fun family times. I find it sobering to realize that every day I am participating in the creation of my children's childhood memories. If you still have time to do something about those memories, don't miss the opportunity.

 Feeling a little blue because your nest is empty this year? Invite a family with young children to a tree-trimming party.

DEBT-PROOF YOUR HOLIDAYS

- If the onslaught of relatives and activities leaves you taking care of everyone but yourself, it may be time to change your holiday habits. Instead of accepting every invitation, take a day—or a few hours—and do something special with your family. Watch a movie, bake a batch of cookies—anything you want to do for a change.

- Start a new tradition. Even though Santa fills all the stockings on Christmas Eve, leave them hanging full and untouched until New Year's Day. This helps to relieve the feeling of overdose on Christmas morning and is a nice way to celebrate the New Year.

- Make miniature Christmas trees for a great holiday family activity. Glue the wide ends of sugar ice-cream cones to a large sheet of cardboard. Spread green icing over the cones and then decorate them with assorted candies like M&M's, gumdrops, Life Savers. Let the kids come up with new decorating ideas for the "Family Forest."

- Little ones will believe Santa was actually in their home if you make boot prints with baking soda. Just dampen the bottom of a pair of boots, dip them into baking soda, and make tracks leading from the chimney to the tree and then to the cookies and milk. Make sure the cookies and milk are properly consumed. The baking soda will vacuum up easily.

Family Fun

🎁 Let your kids turn one of your windows into a holiday canvas. Mix powdered tempera paints (available at an art-supply store or crafts store) with clear dishwashing liquid until they acquire the creamy consistency of house paint. If you have premixed tempera paint, stir in a bit of the dish soap. Use individual plastic containers (margarine tubs are perfect) to mix and separate the colors. Cover the window sash with masking tape and spread newspaper around the surrounding area. Then let the window artists take it away. If you are using a large picture window, help the kids design a mural. Dad and Mom can get into the act by painting the hard-to-reach areas. Windows with individual panes offer a great opportunity for a Christmas montage of a snowflake, a bell, a candy cane, a Christmas tree—one design per pane. When it's completely dry, the paint will come off easily—just wipe with a dry paper towel.

🎁 While sitting around the fire (great reason to turn the television off) one cold winter evening, take turns writing down past events you'd like to forget and toss them into the fireplace.

🎁 Take extra time off work while the kids are out of school for the holidays.

🎁 Make special holiday place mats with your kids. All you need is a box of crayons and light-colored vinyl place mats. Help the kids draw holiday designs and write their name. After the holidays, simply wipe the mats clean with a good all-purpose liquid cleaner. Some traces of color may remain, so make sure you don't use your very best place mats.

- Take an evening for the whole family to prepare and decorate the luminarias (see chapter 11).

- Take the family to see a small-town Christmas parade.

- Take a family holiday photo of the family in the same pose in the same spot, every year.

- Prior to Thanksgiving Day, deliver to each family member who will be in attendance a ticket on which they are to write their current interests, hobbies, and Christmas gift requests. The rule is: No ticket, no dinner. (Make sure they know this is all in fun.)

- Adopt a needy family for the holidays. Make a special shopping trip or have a gift-making session when each member of your family buys or creates a present for the person in the adopted family who is closest to their age.

- Volunteer as a family to work in a soup kitchen or homeless shelter.

- Call a nursing home and get the names of five people who don't often receive mail. Send each one a big holiday card from Santa!

Family Fun

- Take a basket of holiday goodies to your local fire or police station.
- Attach a wreath and big red bow to the front grill of the family car. Hang a fun ornament from the rearview mirror.
- Before going to bed on Christmas Eve, turn out all the lights and light lots of candles. Read the second chapter of Luke, from the Bible, then join hands and sing "Silent Night."
- Tie jingle bells to everyone's sneakers.
- Instead of reading the usual bedtime stories during the month of December, read to your children about Christmas customs in other countries, as well as other wonderful holiday stories available at your local library.
- One night a week during your family's holiday season, eat dinner by the light of the Christmas tree.
- Teach the family to say "Merry Christmas" in a language of the family's origin.
- If you have relatives living far away, videotape your family decorating the house and trimming the tree. Send it to them to enjoy on Christmas Day.
- Get out the board games and have an ongoing family tournament during December.
- If you take your kids to see Santa, here's a way to save time and aggravation shuffling along in long

lines like cattle: stay away from overcrowded malls. Instead, check smaller department stores or neighborhood centers. Santa Claus will probably be visiting in a less hectic atmosphere.

- If the Santa booth allows you to take your own photographs (most do, but be sure to inquire ahead of time) take your own camera when your kids visit with the old gent. Instead of ordering duplicates of the photo, take it to a quick-print place and have colored photocopy enlargements made for about one dollar each.

- Caroling spreads cheer throughout your neighborhood. Bring a thermos of hot cocoa to keep everyone warm.

- Make a wreath from greenery you find in your own backyard and let the children decorate it.

- Bake Christmas cookies for your child's class at school. To save time, make the slice-and-bake variety and decorate them with ready-made frosting.

- On the last day of school before Christmas vacation, tie red and green balloons to the mailbox to welcome your children home.

- Display some great family Christmas pictures from years past in a special photo album or in a location where your family and guests can enjoy them.

Family Fun

🎁 Buy a large white candle (three by eight inches is ideal). Starting at the top, carefully carve twenty-five evenly spaced "stripes" around the candle with the point of a knife. At a designated time each day (dinnertime or bedtime), starting on December 1, light the candle and decide on something you are thankful for as a family. Allow the candle to burn down one stripe each night until Christmas.

🎁 Start a giant jigsaw puzzle at the beginning of the season. The goal is that it be finished by Christmas Day. Keep it out on a table in a well-lit area so that anyone can work on it whenever they want.

🎁 Buy a big candle for the dinner table. Light it every night at dinner during the holidays.

🎁 Reserve opening the day's Christmas cards until dinnertime. Read the messages aloud and remind the kids how the family knows these people.

🎁 Attend a Christmas pageant at your elementary school, even if you do not have children in the school.

🎁 If you are single, getting together with a group of friends who are also single is a great way to celebrate Christmas. How about hosting a work party where everyone pitches in to bake cookies, prepare their cards, and wrap gifts? Some activities are a lot more fun when done in a group. The evening could end with an ornament swap.

- Invite friends over to watch the classic Christmas videos you've rented, like *Frosty the Snowman, A Charlie Brown Christmas, How the Grinch Stole Christmas, Rudolph the Red-Nosed Reindeer, It's a Wonderful Life,* or *Miracle on 34th Street.* Refreshments can be as simple as eggnog and Christmas cookies.

- If you don't have children, make a special trip to the mall just to watch children visit Santa.

- If you find it nearly impossible to gather together all of your married children and families on Christmas Eve or Christmas Day, consider a new tradition of spending the day after Christmas together. This will give you one more day to prepare, and because this is a day typically free from other intrusions, you'll be able to spend a more relaxed time together.

- Take a nighttime walk in your neighborhood to enjoy the holiday lights. It's fun to see decorations up close and personal.

- Go to a recital at a local church. Many choirs perform Handel's *Messiah* and other seasonal favorites.

- Plan a cookie decorating event with your kids. Hint: Bake the cookies early in the day. At party time, set out various toppings and frostings. If you've invited friends, let each child take home a batch of goodies.

🎁 If you have so many in attendance at your Christmas dinners that you must have two tables or more, have everyone get up and exchange places between dinner and dessert.

🎁 On New Year's Eve ask each family member to light a candle and think about the things that happened in the past year for which they are most thankful.

🎁 Save a piece of the Christmas tree trunk to burn as next year's Yule log. Tell the family the legend behind the Yule log. Long ago, people brought home the largest log they could find, usually ash in England and birch in Scotland. They decorated it with a sprig of holly, placed it in the fireplace, and lit it with a piece of the log saved from the previous year. It was hoped that it would burn throughout the twelve days of Christmas. In many households, the lady of the house kept the kindling piece under her pillow. It was thought that this provided year-round protection against fire. If you don't have a fireplace, bring home a festive cake in the shape of a Yule log for Christmas Eve to share with the whole family—or take on a challenge and make a *Bûche de Noël* yourself!

🎁 Give your family a post-Christmas treat by celebrating Twelfth Night on January 6. Also known as the Feast of Epiphany, this Victorian tradition celebrates the day when the three wise men arrived in Bethlehem with their gifts for the Christ child. Children are given three gifts from the Magi before a gala dinner. Afterward, a Twelfth Night cake decorated with figures of kings is served. The child who receives the piece containing the silver coin baked into the cake becomes "king" or "queen" of the family for the whole year!

- Make a "Pin the Red Nose on Rudolph" game board. Draw Rudolph's head on a big sheet of posterboard and cut red noses out of construction paper. Use loops of tape to attach the nose.

- Instead of sending holiday cards to your neighbors, start a new tradition: Organize "The Bentley Street Christmas Book" (or whatever the name of your street or neighborhood). Begin a story (fictional) in a notebook, attach a routing slip with the name of each family on your street, and then send it around the neighborhood with directions for each family to add a sentence or paragraph. When the story comes back to your family, add an appropriate ending. Edit as necessary, print out the story on your computer, and assemble it into a simple book, one for each family that contributed. Have a neighborhood get-together and read the crazy tale. This will bond your neighbors and promote goodwill all through the year.

Family Fun

🎁 Call your local post office to see if they collect letters kids have written to Santa. If they do, have your children pick some out, then select gifts, wrap them, and send them off anonymously. This experience helps teach kids the joy of giving without expecting something in return.

🎁 Carve out a quiet hour or two for a storytelling party with the entire family. Read classic Christmas stories aloud.

🎁 Every Christmas Eve, have your children leave some of their old toys near the fireplace for Santa to take to children who don't have any toys. Once the kids are asleep, hide the toys so you can deliver them to a worthy charity later.

🎁 Don't know how to fill the stockings hanging by the chimney with care? Fill them with stockings! Everyone loves argyles, tube socks, running socks, or knee-highs. Stockings filled with stockings are fun and practical.

🎁 After the tree is undecorated and ready to be thrown out, strip off all the needles. (Make sure you wear gloves.) Then put them into a pillow slip and cover it with a pretty pillow cover. The scent will last all year and will keep the spirit and anticipation of Christmas alive.

Sharing the Joy

There's no better way to share the true spirit of the season than to participate in good deeds. It's a great opportunity to show the kids that Christmas is not just a season for receiving.

If you're not greedy at holidays or throughout the year, your children won't be either. Kids take their cues from their parents. They do what you do, not what you say. If you're in a frenzy, and the holidays are more hassle than happy, the experience will be diminished for your child.

Actions speak louder than words, so when you go caroling at a retirement home, make sandwiches for the homeless, or take toys, clothes, and canned goods to a charity, involve the kids in the entire process to help them understand. Then doing good deeds will become second nature. Here are some other ways your whole family can reach out to others:

- Drive a nondriver to the grocery store, the mall, a holiday service, or a local Christmas program.
- Buy a few extra canned goods each time you go to the grocery store, then donate your surplus to a food bank.
- Participate in an Angel Tree program at a local mall or church. Many charitable organizations decorate a tree with slips of paper, each listing the name, age, sex, and wish list of an underprivileged child. You select a name,

purchase the gift, and bring it back to the tree to be distributed in time for Christmas.

🎁 Take a batch of homemade cookies to a nursing home.

Evaluate

Get the family together during the week after Christmas. Review your holiday plan and the goals you met. Ask everyone what they liked best and least about the holidays and what you'd like to do differently next year. Take notes.

Part IV
One Step Further

All of us who are intimately familiar with overspending know that it is very easy to five-and-ten dollar ourselves into oblivion. The good news is that you can five-and-ten dollar yourself right back to financial health too. The key to rapid debt repayment is to make a plan and stick to it as if your life depended on it. It may. The details of the plan are not nearly as important as your determination to carry it out.

Mary Hunt

The Complete Cheapskate

Chapter 14
A Plan to Wipe Out Debt Forever

Like a lot of people, when McKenzey got her first credit card, she had a feeling of "having arrived," but declared it would be used for emergencies only. A coworker laughed when she heard her say that. Five years later McKenzey had six cards, all maxed out because of "emergencies," and then she understood what had prompted her coworker's chuckle.

Today she owes for car repairs on a car she no longer owns, furniture that she sold in a garage sale, braces that came off her son's teeth a year ago, but worst of all, her balances include several thousand dollars worth of expenses that she doesn't even remember.

Everyone who goes into debt and successfully digs out has a turning point. McKenzey's was facing Christmas buried in bills with no space on any cards. She took a job working for minimum wage in a department store for the holidays.

Her entire Christmas season was miserable because she was exhausted and had no time to enjoy family festivities. But it was such a valuable experience that she now recommends this to anyone sinking into "Credit Card Chaos."

Working in that store, she saw credit from a whole different perspective. Customers would make a small payment on a huge balance, charge twice that while they were in the store, and pay several times as much in the end on already-overpriced merchandise because all they had was their credit line and no cash reserves.

Her customers bought top-of-the-line clothing and housewares as gifts to keep up appearances, but confessed they would never be able to afford these things for themselves. As a cashier, she knew even before they got to the register which customers would charge their purchase; they were the ones with the tired, sad expressions, who were obviously not enjoying the holiday season or anything else. She felt guilty suggesting purchases (the training staff at this store instructed her to suggest the highest-priced options and sell by pushing low payments, never divulging the number of payments) and putting their selections on a charge account because she knew she was helping make their lives worse.

McKenzey felt horrible giving discounts to entice first-time credit-card users because she knew that the merchandise they were buying would not last as long as the payments. The giddy look on the newlyweds' faces when they

A Plan to Wipe Out Debt Forever

first discovered they had more buying power than cash looked sickeningly familiar.

That's the bad news.

The good news is that for the first time in years she made up her mind to get off that merry-go-round forever. She is now going in the opposite direction, out of the hole instead of deeper in. McKenzey is sticking with her Rapid Debt-Repayment Plan and is about halfway to becoming debt-free.

McKenzey told me she's feeling the same things she felt years ago when she got her first credit card: powerful, in charge, secure, and prepared for emergencies. Only this time, her emotions are based in reality.

You've just come through another holiday season. I hope you made it without incurring any new debt. And even if you did, I'm going to assume it was much less than it has been in previous years or what it would have been had you not picked up this book.

If it hasn't already crossed your mind, think about this for a minute: *It is possible to become completely debt-free,* and I'd like to show you how.

You can change the way you deal with money. In just the same way you learned new attitudes about dealing with the holidays, you can learn new money attitudes. Then you can experience the happiness and satisfaction that comes from knowing how to handle your resources in an intelligent and reasoned fashion. Want to give it a try? Well, let's get going.

DEBT-PROOF YOUR HOLIDAYS

First, it is mandatory that you stop incurring new debt and reverse your financially destructive behavior by making a Rapid Debt-Repayment Plan part of your life.

Allow me to introduce you to the rarely-thought-of-and-even-less-enjoyable activity called *debt repayment.* That's a subject the credit card companies don't talk about very often. But I'll give it to you straight: If you ever want to experience financial freedom, peace of mind, and the kind of joy that makes life worth living, somehow, somewhere, sometime you must repay your debts.

If you are relying on your minimum monthly payments to accomplish repayment anytime soon, think again.

Let's say you owe $2,000 on your credit card, which charges 19.8 percent interest for the privilege of using someone else's money. Your minimum monthly payment is 4 percent of the outstanding balance, which is presently about $80 and fluctuates each month depending on the principal balance.

Eighty dollars is all that's required, so that's all you pay, right? Given the typical minimum payment requirements, how long do you think it will take you to pay off that $2,000, even if you never make another purchase? Don't struggle too long with this math challenge. I'll tell you: 116 months. That's almost 10 years, and that's assuming you are never late and never add any new purchases. (Fat chance, huh?) By the time you're finished with the payment plan designed by the credit card company, you will have paid interest in the amount of $1,215.44. And if you are a typical consumer, i.e., a preferred and valued customer, meaning you keep your credit cards "maxed out" or at least make sure there's a good, healthy balance rolling over from month to month, it is highly unlikely your consumer debt will ever be paid off. This, my friend, is what I call *perma-debt,* and the credit card companies love it.

Let's go back to that $2,000 debt example, which has a current monthly minimum payment of $80. What if through some stroke of unexplained sense you made a solemn and personal pledge to pay $80 every month until the darned thing was paid in full, choosing to ignore the fact that the actual monthly minimum payment requirement was decreasing every month? You would reach a zero balance in just 32 months instead of 116. And if you got real sane and committed to pay $90 a month? Then the debt would be history in just 28 months. Brace yourself, but let's assume you really lost your mind and you made a personal pledge to pay $100 a month against this $2,000 debt. You would pay it off in just 24 months, more than *eight years sooner* than if you believed the credit card company when they said all you have to pay is the minimum monthly balance. I never cease to be amazed by the power of compounded interest and what it can do to one's financial picture!

DEBT-PROOF YOUR HOLIDAYS

All of us who are intimately familiar with overspending know that it is easy to five-and-ten dollar ourselves into oblivion. The good news is that you can five-and-ten dollar yourself right back to financial health too.

The key to rapid debt repayment is to make a plan and then stick to it as if your life depends on it. The details of the plan for your own debt reduction are not nearly as important as your determination to carry it out.

There are several methods of rapid debt reduction that work equally well. One method involves a plan whereby each of one's debts are paid off proportionately so that they all reach zero balance at the same time.

However, the method that I will teach you and which is, coincidentally, my personal favorite, is based on the principle that it brings a great deal of personal gratification (we overspenders are really into gratification—and the instant kind is the best) to work extra hard on one bill at a time in order to experience the exhilaration of a zero balance as quickly as possible.

Paying off one debt completely gives a great boost to your determination to pay the next and the next and the next. While not instant gratification, this method certainly offers short-term achievable goals. Small dosages of gratification along the way keep me motivated, that's for sure. Here's how it works:

The first thing you must do is determine exactly how much you owe and the exact nature of your debts. We are talking

A Plan to Wipe Out Debt Forever

about unsecured debt, which includes credit card balances, personal loans, payments you are making to the dentist or doctor, anything that you owe but would not be subject to repossession if you stopped paying. Include all of your unsecured debts.

Make a written list that includes the current balance, minimum payment, interest rate, and number of payments required to pay it in full. If you do not possess the math skills required to figure how many payments will be required to pay the debt off at the current terms, you might consider using a financial calculator or call the creditor and ask. Some creditors will not help you with this information, particularly if you have a variable interest rate. In that case, go to your bank or call a math teacher. If you are a little confused, here is the question you should ask: "With my present balance of $$$ [insert your current balance] how many months will it take me to pay this debt in full if I make a monthly payment of $$ [insert your present minimum monthly payment] every month and add no new purchases?"

Next, arrange your debts in order of the number of months required to pay in full, with the shortest payoff first on the list. (See Mr. and Mrs. Example's plan that follows.) The debt that they placed first on the list has a balance of $80. With a minimum payment of $35, it will take just a bit longer than two months to pay it off, which is less than any of their debts. Next, add up the total of the current minimum monthly payments.

DEBT-PROOF YOUR HOLIDAYS

This is a very important number, so write it down, embed it in your brain, tattoo it on your forehead, paint it on your walls, teach it to your children. Forgive me, I go a little nuts now and again. You can skip the tattoo.

And now, *it's commitment time.* In the same way you made a personal commitment to not incur holiday debts, you need to make a personal commitment that until you are debt-free you will pay the same amount toward your debts every month until they are paid off.

Look again at the total of your minimum monthly payments, that number you've just embedded in your brain. This is the amount of money you must commit to pay toward your Rapid Debt-Repayment Plan until all of your debts are paid. You shouldn't find this at all out of line because this is the amount you have to pay every month whether you ever picked up this book or not. At this point I am not asking you to pay any more than you are required to pay. (It wouldn't be such a bad idea, but it's not required.) This is the minimum amount you must devote to your Rapid Debt-Repayment Plan regardless of the minimum amount the creditor says you owe in one particular month decreasing or not. Remember, they want you to pay less every month so you can keep paying forever.

Look at the Rapid Debt-Repayment Plan example on pages 158 and 159. Basically this is how it works: The total of the minimum monthly payments in the first month is $619.

A Plan to Wipe Out Debt Forever

This is the amount our Example family has committed to pay every month until they are debt-free, regardless of anything their creditors say about lower payments. In Month 1, the Examples make all of the minimum monthly payments for a total of $619. In Month 2 they do the very same thing. In Month 3, they make their committed payments just like in the past two months—except, the payment to Department Store 1 is only $12 because that is the total outstanding balance. Wow! The first zero balance. So what happens to the $23 they didn't have to send to Department Store 1 because of the zero balance? Should they use it to celebrate the first victory? No! That $23 must be included with the regular payment to Personal Loan (the next debt in line), increasing its payment of $108 to $131.

In Month 4 the $35 payment that used to go to Department Store 1 is now added to Personal Loan's payment so it becomes $143. This additional payment (technically prepayment of the principle) is what will get Personal Loan paid in just seven months, including interest. The total amount paid in Month 4 is still $619 even though the number of debts has been reduced.

Now look at what happened to Student Loan while this was going on. It reached a zero balance in Month 4 as well, so now three debts are completely paid off. But since the Examples are committed to paying $619 every month against their debts, the payment to Visa 1 is substantially

RAPID DEBT-REPAYMENT PLAN

Creditor	$ Balance	%	1	2	3	4	5	6	7	8	9	
Dept. Store 1	80	16.9%	35	35	12	0						
Personal Loan	700	10%	108	108								
Student Loan	200	6%	26	26	26	26	26	74	0			
Visa 1	1,500	18%	108	108	108	108	108	114	277	277	277	
Orthodontist	3,000	18%	40	40	40	40	40	40	40	40	40	
Credit Union	3,000	12%	120	120	120	120	120	120	120	120	120	
Finance Co.	1,200	14%	45	45	45	45	45	45	45	45	45	
MasterCard	1,000	19.6%	40	40	40	40	40	40	40	40	40	
Visa 2	650	18%	32	32	32	32	32	32	32	32	32	
Dept. Store 2	2,000	18.5%	65	65	65	65	65	65	65	65	65	
Totals	$11,330		619	619	619	619	619	619	619	619	619	

A Plan to Wipe Out Debt Forever

10	11	12	13	14	15	16	17	18	19	20	21	22	23	24	25	26	27
								(Debt-free in just 24 months ↗)									
227	209	0															
40	108	385	369	0													
120	120	120	136	437	437	437	437	437	145	0							
45	45	45	45	45	45	45	45	45	337	278							
40	40	40	40	40	40	40	40	40	40	244	264	0					
32	32	32	32	32	32	32	32	32	32	32	128	0					
65	65	65	65	65	65	65	65	65	65	65	227	619	519	0			
619	619	619	619	619	619	619	619	619	619	619	619	619	519		DEBT-FREE!		

increased because the old payments for Department Store 1,
Personal Loan, and Student Loan are all added to the Visa 1
payment, increasing it from $108 to $227 until it is fully paid
in Month 11.

And on it goes. The Examples pay $619 every month,
always taking the old payments and adding them to the payment of the next debt in line until they are 100 percent debt-
free in Month 23! You must agree that this is truly amazing,
considering that given the slow-pay method, Sam and
Samantha would have been paying on these debts for 12
years or more, provided of course that they never missed a
payment and did not incur any new debt.

To recap, here are the five steps for wiping out your
debts in record time:

1. *You must repent.* Relax. *Repent* simply means to turn
   around and go in a different direction. You must repent
   from *debting,* that is, incurring new debts. If you don't
   complete this first step, the plan will not work.

2. *You must pay the same amount every month
   until all of your unsecured debts are paid in full.*
   From this moment on, you must adopt the total of
   your current minimum monthly payments as your
   regular monthly obligation, not unlike your house or
   car payment. It will not change from month to
   month. It's big, it's ugly, and it's not going away. Just
   accept it.

3. *List your debts in order according to the number of months left.* For example, a debt to a department store of $80 total with a minimum monthly payment of $40 has about two months left (the total paid will be slightly higher than the $80 because of the interest). That one goes at the top of your list.

4. *From here on out ignore declining minimum monthly payments.* Whatever the minimum is in the first month is the amount you are going to pay until your total debt is wiped out, regardless of whether the creditor shows a lower amount due on your statement.

5. *As one debt is paid off, apply its monthly payment to the next debt.* No matter how many debts you have paid off, you must commit to pay the same total amount every month until every debt is paid.

If you want to see your Rapid Debt-Repayment Plan work even more quickly, increase your monthly commitment.

Remember: the key to repaying debt quickly is to prepay the principal.

Afterword

Well, our time to think and dream about Christmas has just about come to a close. I'm excited! How about you?

I believe that the timing of our lives is unique. The time was right for me to write this book; the time was right for you to read it.

As you begin preparations for the holidays, my prayer for you is that you will go through the season with a clear sense of what you value, that you will have the courage to celebrate in meaningful ways that fill your soul and connect you with something much larger than yourself, and that you will never again dread the most wonderful time of the year.

As you discover new and wonderful ways to debt-proof your holidays, please let me hear about them. I want to know about your struggles, solutions, and successes. Please understand that while I read all of my mail, it is not always possible for me to send a personal reply.

> Mary Hunt
> P.O. Box 2135
> Paramount, CA 90723-8135

May your days be merry and bright . . . and may all your Christmases be *debt-free!*

Endnotes

1. *CardTrak* (March 1997). *CardTrak* is a newsletter published by CardWeb Inc., P.O. Box 3966, 1270 Fairfield Road, Suite 51, Gettysburg, Pennsylvania 17325, http://www.cardtrak.com. Annual subscription for twelve issues is $59.

2. *CardTrak* (December 1996).

3. Joe Robinson and Jean Coppock Staeheli, *Unplug the Christmas Machine* (New York: Quill Books, a division of William Morrow and Company, 1991), 104.

A Special Offer

What Is
Cheapskate Montbly?

Cheapskate Montbly is a twelve-page newsletter published twelve times a year. It is dedicated to helping those who are struggling to live within their means find practical and realistic solutions to their financial problems. *Cheapskate Montbly* provides hope, encouragement, inspiration, and motivation to individuals who are committed to financially responsible and debt-free living and provides the highest quality information and resources possible in a format exclusive of paid advertising. You will find *Cheapskate Montbly* filled with tips, humor, and just plain great information to help you stretch your dollars.

How to subscribe:
Send check or money order for $18 to:
Cheapskate Montbly
P.O. Box 2135, Paramount, CA 90723-8135
(562) 630-8845 for information only
(800) 550-3502 for phone orders only
http://www.cheapskatemonthly.com
(Please call for Canadian and foreign rates)

SPECIAL OFFER:
Enclose this original coupon with your check or money order, and your one-year subscription to *Cheapskate Montbly* will be extended for an additional three months. That's 15 months for the price of 12. Such a deal, considering $18 for 12 full issues is already cheap!
(Subscription rate subject to change without notice.)

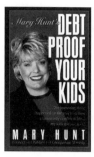

More great resources for DEBT-FREE LIVING

THE FINANCIALLY CONFIDENT WOMAN

The Financially Confident Woman tells the story of Mary's journey to the brink of financial disaster and back. She documents the hidden dangers of easy credit, shows women how to control their financial futures, identifies nine characteristics of financially confident women, and offers detailed plans for turning bad financial habits around and putting sound financial principles into action!
Trade Paper 0-8054-6285-6
Audio Book (read by the author) 0-8054-8378-0

THE FINANCIALLY CONFIDENT WOMAN PERPETUAL CALENDAR

0-8054-0008-7

THE FINANCIALLY CONFIDENT WOMAN MINI BOOK

0-8054-6300-3

available at fine bookstores everywhere

Could you live in a house that didn't stay still?

Homes That Move

the
BIG
PICTURE

Angela Royston

First Facts is published by Capstone Press, a Capstone imprint,
151 Good Counsel Drive, P.O. Box 669, Mankato, Minnesota 56002.
www.capstonepub.com

First published in 2010 by A&C Black Publishers Limited, 36 Soho Square, London W1D 3QY
www.acblack.com
Copyright © A&C Black Ltd. 2010

Produced for A&C Black by Calcium. www.calciumcreative.co.uk

042010
005769ACS11

Library of Congress Cataloging-in-Publication Data
Royston, Angela, 1945-
  Homes that move / by Angela Royston.
    p. cm. — (First Facts, The big picture)
  Includes bibliographical references and index.
  ISBN 978-1-4296-5527-9 (library binding)
  ISBN 978-1-4296-5528-6 (paperback)
  1. Dwellings—Juvenile literature. 2. Mobile homes—Juvenile
literature. I. Title. II. Series.

  GT172.R69 2011
  392.3'6—dc22   2010015737

Every effort has been made to trace copyright holders and to obtain their permission for use of copyright material.
This book is produced using paper that is made from wood grown in managed, sustainable forests. It is natural,
renewable and recyclable. The logging and manufacturing processes conform to the environmental regulations
of the country of origin.

Acknowledgements

The publishers would like to thank the following for their kind permission to reproduce their photographs:

Cover: Istockphoto: Simon Gurney (front), Shutterstock: Styve Reineck (back). **Pages:** Fotolia: Thomas Pozzo di
Borgo 1; Istockphoto: Chris Leachman 19, Andrew Penner 18-19; Photolibrary: Age Fotostock 14-15; Shutterstock:
Diego Cervo 21, Ant Clausen 20-21, Elena Elisseeva 16-17, Hironai 16, Lana 2-3, Dave McAleavy 8-9, 22-23,
Vladimir Melnik 6-7, Caitlin Mirra 4-5, Monkey Business Images 4-5, Mikhail Nekrasov 12-13, Tyler Olson 14-15,
Styve Reineck 6, Steve Rosset 24, s74 12-13, Kulaeva Tamara 10-11, 11, Aleksandar Todorovic 8-9, TOSP Photo 3.

Printed in the United States of America in Stevens Point, Wisconsin.
062011   006273

Contents

Homes 4

Tent House 6

Houseboat.................................. 8

Raft House................................ 10

Stilt House 12

Tree House 14

Sky Home 16

On Wheels 18

Holiday House......................... 20

Glossary 22

Further Reading 23

Index 24

Homes

Most people live in homes that do not move. They live in houses or flats that stay still.

Moving houses

Some people need to live in houses that can move. They take the houses with them as they travel.

When most people move, they do not move their house with them!

4

Air, land, water

Some people live in very wet places. They need houses that can move on water, or sway in trees high up above the water below.

Moving house

Tent House

Nomads **are people who live in tents, which they carry with them wherever they go.**

Follow the animals

Nomads keep animals such as camels and goats. When the animals move to find food, the nomads go with them.

*Many nomads live in hot **deserts**.*

6

Hot and cold

Some nomads live in hot places where there are deserts. Others live in grassy places where it can be cold.

Let's go!

Houseboat

A houseboat is a boat that people live on. It has rooms for sleeping and for cooking.

All year round

Some people live on houseboats all the time. They tie up their boat on the **waterway**, or in a **harbour**.

Chug, chug!

Just holidays

Some houseboats are used just for holidays. People use them to travel slowly along rivers, lakes, or **canals**.

Many houseboats are painted bright colours.

9

Raft House

Some people live in floating homes. There are even floating villages! They move from side to side in the water.

All aboard

A floating village has no roads and no cars or trucks. Everything is brought to the village by boat.

Floating villages are built on **rafts**.

Fish food

The people in this floating village catch fish. They sell some of the fish to people on the land.

Keep paddling!

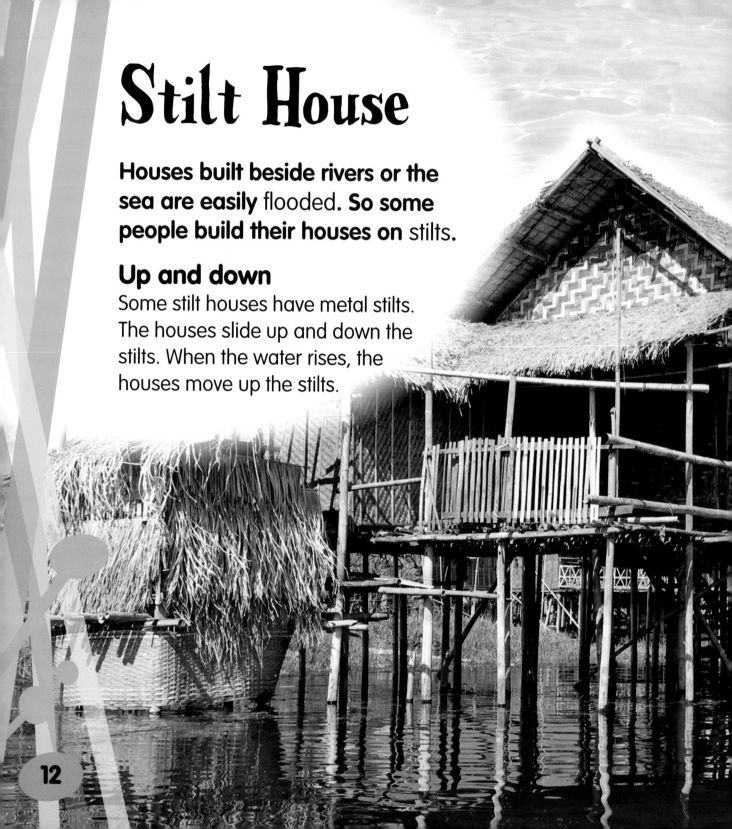

Stilt House

Houses built beside rivers or the sea are easily flooded. **So some people build their houses on** stilts.

Up and down

Some stilt houses have metal stilts. The houses slide up and down the stilts. When the water rises, the houses move up the stilts.

High and dry

Strong stilts

The stilts on houses are so strong that they do not move in the flowing water. The house on top stays still and dry.

These stilt houses are made of wood.

Tree House

How would you like to live at the top of a tree? Some people build their houses there.

No water up here!

The Korowai people live in **swamps** that often flood, so they build their houses high up in the trees. The houses sway in the wind with the trees.

It's a long climb to the front door!

Tree trip

Some **wildlife parks** have tree houses. Visitors can sleep safely in the trees, away from wild animals below.

Don't look down!

Sky Home

Homes at the top of skyscrapers **are higher above the ground than any other home.**

Are we moving?
A skyscraper is built to sway in strong winds, although people may not feel it moving.

Sky high!

16

Don't move!

Very tall buildings are sometimes built with heavy water tanks on top. This stops the buildings from moving too much.

You get a bird's eye view from the top of a skyscraper.

On Wheels

Caravans and camper vans **are homes that people can drive from place to place.**

Pull or drive?

Camper vans have an engine, so they can be driven. Caravans do not have engines, so must be pulled by a car.

On the road

Gypsy caravans are often painted with bright colours.

Gypsy house

Gypsies and travellers live in caravans all year round. They used to travel in their caravan from place to place, but today they usually stay in a special campsite.

Holiday House

Have you ever slept in a tent? Lots of people live in a tent when they go on holiday.

Home in a minute

You can take a tent anywhere you are allowed to camp. Most tents fit over a metal frame and are easy to put up.

Holiday time

Sleep and eat

Campers usually cook food on a barbeque or on a small **gas stove**. They zip themselves into a sleeping bag at night.

Camping can be a lot of fun.

Glossary

camper vans vans you can live in

canals waterways that boats travel on

deserts dusty, dry, and rocky places

flooded covered with water

gas stove small cooker powered by gas

gypsies people who travel and live in caravans

harbour area by the sea where boats are kept

nomads people who travel with their animals

rafts lengths of wood tied together

skyscrapers tallest type of buildings

stilts tall poles that hold up a house on top

swamps watery places with very soggy ground

waterway river or canal boats travel along
such as a river or canal

wildlife parks places people can visit to
see animals in the wild

Further Reading

Websites

See more photographs of stilt houses at:
www.visualgeography.com/categories/thailand/houses

Look at some great tree house pictures at:
www.weburbanist.com/2008/02/10/10-amazing-tree-houses-from-around-the-world-sustainable-unique-and-creative-designs/

Click on Homes to find different games about houses at:
www.bbc.co.uk/schools/websites/4_11/site/geography

Books

Homes (Starters) by Rosie McCormick, Wayland (2005).

Homes on the Move (Homes Around the World) by Nicola Barber, Wayland (2007).

Index

animals 6, 15

boats 8–9, 10

camper vans 18–19
canals 9
caravans 18–19
cooking 8, 20

deserts 6, 7

fish 11
floating villages 10–11
flooded 12, 14

gas stove 20
gypsies 19

harbour 8
holidays 9, 20–21
houseboats 8–9

Korowai 14

nomads 6–7

rafts 10–11

skyscrapers 16–17
stilts 12–13
swamps 14

tents 6, 20
tree houses 14–15

water 5, 8–9, 10–11, 12–13
waterway 8
wildlife parks 15
winds 16